MULTICULTURAL COOKBOOK

Authentic Recipes from 117 Countries

Semra N. Yüksel

BREAKWATER

TO MY SON ARDA

Breakwater
100 Water Street
P.O. Box 2188
St. John's, Newfoundland
A1C 6E6

Canadian Cataloguing in Publication Data

Yüksel, Semra N., 1948

Multicultural cookbook

ISBN 1-55081-016-2

1. Cookery, International. I. Title

TX725.A1Y85 1992 C92-098532-7

Copyright © 1992 Semra N. Yüksel

Printed in Canada.

Table of Contents

Abbreviations

c	cup
cm	centimetre
C	degree Celsius
F	degree Fahrenheit
g	gram
kg	kilogram
L	litre
lb	pound
mL	millilitre
oz	ounce
qt	pint
T	tablespoon
t	teaspoon

Foreword

Through my interest in and involvement with multiculturalism, I have discovered how food is the icebreaker for communication and exchange between individuals from different ethnic backgrounds, and how curious people are about ethnic cooking. At Canada Day events, it is common to see people tasting various foods, comparing notes and sharing recipes. I also experienced that food almost always produced a warm, informal atmosphere.

Having travelled to many countries and been involved with studying and promoting the cultural values of those countries, I found myself possessing interesting recipes and a keen interest in all kinds of cooking.

The combination of a genuine and growing interest among Canadians in exploring the food of ethnic groups, my interest in cultural diversities, and my possession of many ethnic recipes drove me to do more research in this area. As a result of four years of research I have compiled a *MULTI-CULTURAL COOKBOOK* which contains recipes from 117 countries.

The material is arranged by country, with a brief and informative sketch of the country preceding each recipe. This will give people a cognitive link to each country as well as the taste of the food. All recipes are typical and they range from the simplest to the most complex. The cooking techniques are clear, simple and easily workable in any modern or conventional kitchen.

I have no doubt that this cookbook is one aspect of our cultural heritage and as Canada becomes increasingly a multicultural society, food will continue to play an important bridging role between ethnic communities. Not only will mealtimes bring families together, but communities will be brought closer in spirit.

SEMRA N. YÜKSEL

Acknowledgements

I would like to express my appreciation to all the people in Canada and all around the world who provided me with recipes, advice and useful hints, while I was collecting recipes. If it were not for them, this book could never be realized.

I also greatly appreciate the cooperation of the following countries: Algeria, Australia, Austria, Belgium, Chile, Cuba, Czechoslovakia, Denmark, Ecuador, Finland, Federal Republic of Germany, Ghana, Greece, Guyana, Hungary, India, Iraq, Ireland, Japan, Jordan, Kuwait, Lesotho, Mauritania, Morocco, Netherlands, New Zealand, Nigeria, Norway, Philippines, Republic of South Africa, Spain, Sweden, Switzerland, Syria, Tanzania, Yugoslavia.

Finally, I would like to thank my husband for his invaluable support and his unending patience.

AFGHANISTAN

Location:	Asia
Capital City:	Kabul
Language:	Pushtu, Dari Persian
Monetary Unit:	Afghani

AFGHANI PUDDING
Servings: 4

Ingredients:

500	mL	2	c	milk
125	mL	½ c		sugar
30	mL	2	T	cornstarch
45	mL	3	T	rice flour
125	mL	½ c		water
60	mL	¼ c		pistachio nuts, chopped
				dash of salt

Method:

1. Place milk, sugar and salt in a double boiler. Bring to boiling point.

2. In a cup, mix cornstarch and rice flour. Stir in water slowly until smooth. Gradually add mixture to boiling milk. Stir constantly. Cook over low heat about 15 minutes or until pudding mixture thickens.

3. Pour hot pudding into cups. Chill. Before serving sprinkle with pistachio nuts.

ALBANIA

Location: Europe
Capital City: Tirana
Language: Albanian
Monetary Unit: Lek

LEEK WITH RICE
Servings: 6

Ingredients:

1	kg	2	lb	leek
125	mL	½	c	olive oil
30	mL	⅛	c	onion, finely chopped
125	mL	½	c	carrot, scraped, sliced
5	mL	1	t	tomato pure
60	mL	¼	c	converted rice
500	mL	2	c	water
15	mL	1	T	sugar
				salt
1		1		lemon

Method:

1. Saute onions, carrots and leeks in oil (cut leeks in 2 cm / 1 inch pieces, using only white and light green parts). Add tomato puree and 1 cup of water, mix well. Cover and cook about 20 minutes over low heat.

2. Add remaining water, sugar, juice of half a lemon and salt. Bring to a boil. Sprinkle in rice, reduce heat again, cover and cook until water is absorbed.

3. Place on serving plate, chill. Decorate with lemon wedges.

ALGERIA

Location: Africa
Capital City: Algiers
Language: Arabic, French
Monetary Unit: Dinar

EGGPLANT CASSEROLE
Servings: 2

Ingredients:

500	g	1	lb	meat, cubed
1		1		large tomato, chopped
1		1		Spanish onion, chopped
3		3		garlic cloves, crushed
5	mL	1	t	caraway seeds
45	mL	3	T	margarine
				salt
				black pepper
				water
1		1		large eggplant, sliced
125	mL	½ c		oil
				parsley leaves, chopped

Method:

1. Saute meat and onion in margarine until light brown. Add salt, pepper and water (enough to cover). Cook over medium heat until partially cooked.

2. Add garlic and caraway. Reduce heat, cook until meat is tender.

3. Meanwhile fry eggplant slices. When light brown remove from pan and drain.

4. Place meat mixture in a casserole dish, cover with fried eggplant, sprinkle with parsley and serve hot.

ANTIGUA AND BARBUDA

Location: Lesser Antilles
Capital City: Saint John's
Language: English
Monetary Unit: East Caribbean Dollar

GINGER BEER
Servings: 4

Ingredients:

1 L	4 c	water
30 mL	⅛ c	fresh ginger, grated
		sugar
		vanilla essence

Method:

1. Cover ginger with water overnight.

2. Strain through coffee filter.

3. Add sugar and vanilla essence to taste. If too strong, add more water.

4. Bottle and store in refrigerator.

ARGENTINA

Location: South America
Capital City: Buenos Aires
Language: Spanish
Monetary Unit: Austrol

MEAT TURNOVERS
Servings: 10

Ingredients:

750	mL	3	c	flour
5	mL	1	t	salt
2	mL	½	t	baking powder
1		1		egg yolk
125	mL	½	c	butter, at room temperature
5	mL	1	t	vinegar
125	mL	½	c	water
3		3		onions, finely chopped
2		2		garlic cloves, finely chopped
2		2		green pepper, finely chopped
1		1		large tomato, finely chopped
45	mL	3	T	oil
250	g	½	lb	lean ground meat
2	mL	½	t	chili powder
2	mL	½	t	black pepper
5	mL	1	t	salt
5	mL	1	t	sugar
15	mL	1	T	flour
2		2		eggs, hard boiled
8		8		black olives, pitted, quartered

Method:

1. FOR PASTRY: Combine flour, sugar, salt and baking powder. Blend well. Work butter in with fingertips until mixture resembles course meal. Place on a board and make a depression in the centre of the mixture.

2. Combine water, egg yolk and vinegar in a small bowl and beat well.

3. Add all of liquid mixture at once to the depression in the pastry. Stir with fork until dough holds together. Wrap and chill.

4. FOR FILLING: Saute onions, garlic and meat in oil until golden brown. Add green pepper and tomato, cook several minutes, then add seasonings and flour. Simmer for 15 minutes, stirring occasionally. When cooked let it cool.

ARGENTINA (Continued)

5. Roll chilled dough into circles 0.3 cm (⅛ inch) thick and about 13 cm (5 inch) in diameter.

6. Place about 30 mL (⅛ c) of filling on each pastry round; top with slices of egg and olive.

7. Wet edges of pastry with water. Fold over and press edges to seal. Prick the top with a fork. Brush with an egg yolk diluted in a little water.

8. Place on an ungreased baking sheet and bake in a preheated oven at 200°C (400°F) to a rich brown, about 15 minutes.

AUSTRALIA

Location:	Oceania
Capital City:	Canberra
Language:	English
Monetary Unit:	Australian Dollar

PAPAYA WEDGES
Servings: 4

Ingredients:

1		1		ripe papaya
1		1		packet lemon jello
250	mL	1	c	orange juice
250	mL	1	c	boiling water
15	mL	1	T	sherry
4		4		kiwi

Method:

1. Cut papaya in halves lengthwise, scoop out seeds. Add sherry and set aside.

2. Dissolve jelly powder in boiling water, then add orange juice. Chill until set, then beat well until light and fluffy. Combine with kiwi and sherry and the juice collected in the papaya. Mix well.

3. Divide the mixture between the two halves of the papaya. Chill until jelly is set firmly.

4. When ready, cut each half in two wedges, serve with ice cream.

AUSTRALIA (Continued)

PINEAPPLE SURPRISE
Servings: 4

Ingredients:

2		2		small pineapples
3		3		bananas, peeled, sliced
60	mL	4	T	butter, unsalted
60	mL	4	T	sugar
125	mL	½	c	cognac
250	mL	1	c	orange sherbet

Method:

1. Cut pineapples in half lengthwise. Cut out the pulp and dice it. Reserve the shells.

2. Melt butter, stir in sugar. Add diced pineapple and bananas. Stir gently. Cook one minute.

3. Warm the cognac, set it aflame and pour over fruit. When flame dies, stuff pineapple shells with fruit mixture and top each shell with 60 mL (¼ c) of orange sherbet.

AUSTRIA

Location:	Europe
Capital City:	Vienna
Language:	German
Monetary Unit:	Schilling

SHRIMP VIENNESE STYLE
Servings: 6

Ingredients:

1	kg	2	lb	shrimp
2		2		shallots, finely chopped
60	mL	¼	c	oil
60	mL	¼	c	brandy
125	mL	½	c	white wine
				dash of sugar
15	mL	1	T	butter
5	mL	1	t	flour
15	mL	1	T	tomato puree
				salt
				cayenne pepper

Method:

1. Remove shells and veins from shrimp.

2. Fry shallots in oil, add shrimp. Pour brandy over mixture and set aflame. When flame has burned down, add white sugar, tomato puree, salt and cayenne pepper. Simmer 15 minutes, then remove shrimp.

3. In a small pan, melt butter, blend in flour, stir until golden. Add 15 mL (1 T) shrimp gravy (above) and stir. Add remainder of gravy and bring to a boil. If necessary, strain.

4. Add shrimp to the sauce, heat gently.

BANGLADESH

Location:	Asia
Capital City:	Dhaka
Language:	Bengali, English
Monetary Unit:	Taka

BENGALI CHICKEN CURRY
Servings: 6

Ingredients:

1		*1*		*chicken, skinned, jointed*
				paprika
				salt
45	*mL*	*3*	*T*	*oil*
2		*2*		*onions, finely chopped*
2		*2*		*garlic cloves, crushed*
250	*mL*	*1*	*c*	*tomatoes, chopped*
125	*mL*	*½*	*c*	*water*
2	*mL*	*½*	*t*	*chili powder*
2	*mL*	*½*	*t*	*dried mustard*
2	*mL*	*½*	*t*	*turmeric*
2	*mL*	*½*	*t*	*ground cardamom*
2	*mL*	*½*	*t*	*ground cinnamon*
2	*mL*	*½*	*t*	*cumin*
5	*mL*	*1*	*t*	*ground coriander*

Method:

1. Sprinkle chicken pieces with a little paprika and salt. Brown each piece in oil for 10 minutes. Remove and keep warm.

2. In the same oil, fry onions, garlic, cardamom and cinnamon. When onions are golden brown, add all the other spices. Cook slowly for about 5 minutes. Then add tomatoes and water and simmer for 15 minutes.

3. Empty the skillet into a bowl. Replace chicken pieces, sprinkle with a little salt, then pour the curry sauce over the chicken. Cover pan and simmer over low heat for 45 minutes or until chicken is tender.

BARBADOS

Location:	Caribbeans
Capital City:	Bridgetown
Language:	English
Monetary Unit:	Barbados Dollar

BEAN RICE
Servings: 4

Ingredients:

2		2	green onions, chopped
1		1	clove garlic, chopped
4		4	parsley sprigs, chopped
1	mL	¼ t	thyme
			salt
45	mL	3 T	peanut oil
500	mL	2 c	converted rice
375	mL	1 ½ c	red beans, cooked
500	mL	2 c	water

Method:

1. Heat oil and seasoning (onions, garlic, parsley, thyme and salt) over medium heat. Add rice and stir until rice is coated with oil.

2. Add water, bring to a boil. Add beans, mix well. Cover, reduce heat to a very low degree and cook undisturbed for about 15 minutes. Remove cover, stir, replace cover and cook 10 more minutes or until all liquid is absorbed.

BELGIUM

Location:	Europe
Capital City:	Brussels
Language:	Flemish, French
Monetary Unit:	Belgian Franc

RABBIT WITH PRUNES
Servings: 2

Ingredients:

2		2		rabbit legs
45	mL	3	T	butter
1		1		Spanish onion, finely sliced
15	mL	1	T	flour
375	mL	1 ½ c		red wine
7	mL	½ T		sugar
2	mL	½ t		wine vinegar
180	mL	¾ c		prunes, dry

Method:

1. Soak prunes in cold water for 2 hours.

2. Brown rabbit legs in butter. Remove from heat and place in saucepan.

3. Fry onions in the same butter, sprinkle with flour. Mix well and add wine. Bring to a boil, stirring constantly.

4. Place rabbit legs in sauce, then add sugar, vinegar and prunes. Cook covered over low heat for 75 minutes.

5. Remove legs from sauce, place on a platter, arrange prunes around legs and pour sauce over top.

 **BOLIVIA**

Location:	South America
Capital City:	Sucre
Language:	Spanish, Quechua, Aymara
Monetary Unit:	Boliviano

BAKED CORN
Servings: 4

Ingredients:

250	mL	1	c	Spanish onion, sliced
500	gr	1	lb	round beef, cubed
30	mL	2	T	flour
1	mL	¼	t	chili powder
1	mL	¼	t	black pepper
2	mL	½	t	salt
125	mL	½	c	tomatoes, chopped
60	mL	4	T	oil
500	mL	2	c	water
250	mL	1	c	corn kernels, fresh or canned
1		1		egg, beaten
15	mL	1	T	milk
60	gr	⅛	lb	goat's milk cheese, grated

Method:

1. Dip beef into flour. Saute in oil until slightly brown, add onions, turning frequently.

2. Stir in chili powder, black pepper and salt. Mix well, then add tomatoes and water. Simmer 30 minutes or until beef is tender.

3. Pour meat mixture in 23 x 23 x 5 cm (9 x 9 x 2 inch) baking dish. Set aside.

4. Combine corn with egg, milk and cheese mixture. Pour over meat.

5. Bake at 180°C (350°F) about 1 hour.

BRAZIL

Location:	South America
Capital City:	Brasilia
Language:	Portuguese
Monetary Unit:	Cruzado

FISH AND SHRIMP STEW
Servings: 4

Ingredients:

1		1		Spanish onion, chopped
1		1		garlic clove, minced
45	mL	3	T	oil
2	mL	½	t	chili powder
2	mL	½	t	paprika
7	mL	½	T	ground coriander seed
				salt
4		4		medium tomatoes, quartered
250	mL	1	c	water
25	g	½	lb	shrimp, shelled, deveined
50	g	1	lb	flounder fillets

Method:

1. Saute onions and garlic in oil until golden. Add chili powder, paprika, ground coriander seed, salt, tomatoes and shrimp. Simmer, stirring occasionally, for 5 minutes.

2. Place large pieces of fish in shrimp mixture and mix gently. Add water, bring to a boil. Lower heat, cover and simmer 20 minutes.

BULGARIA

Location:	Europe
Capital City:	Sofia
Language:	Bulgarian, Turkish
Monetary Unit:	Lev

MUTTON TONGUES
Servings: 4

Ingredients:

2		2		mutton tongues
1		1		Spanish onion, chopped
2		2		medium carrots, sliced
30	mL	2	T	white wine
900	g	2	lb	potatoes, sliced
60	mL	4	T	oil
				black pepper
				salt
500	mL	2	c	water

Method:

1. Cook tongues in salted water until tender. Remove skin and fry tongues in oil to light golden brown. Remove from pan.

2. In the same pan fry onion. When light brown, add carrots and saute until onions are golden brown. Add wine, salt, black pepper and water. Cover and simmer 5 minutes.

3. In a fireproof casserole dish, place mixture of potato and tongue slices. Pour in the simmered onion mixture.

4. Bake at 180°C (350°F) for 30 minutes.

BURMA

Location: Asia
Capital City: Yangon
Language: Burmese
Monetary Unit: Kyat

BURMESE BEEF CURRY
Servings: 4

Ingredients:

500	*g*	*1*	*lb*		*lean stew beef*
2		*2*			*garlic cloves, minced*
2		*2*			*medium onions, chopped*
60	*mL*	*¼*	*c*		*oil*
2	*mL*	*½*	*t*		*ground ginger*
2	*mL*	*½*	*t*		*chili powder*
15	*mL*	*1*	*T*		*curry powder*
3		*3*			*tomatoes, chopped*
10	*mL*	*2*	*t*		*salt*
1		*1*			*juice of lemon*
500	*g*	*1*	*lb*		*baby potatoes, scraped*
500	*mL*	*2*	*c*		*water*

Method:

1. Fry onions and garlic in oil. Add curry powder. Stir and fry for about 10 minutes.

2. Add meat, mix well and cook for 10 more minutes. Then add tomatoes and water. Bring to a boil. Cover pan and simmer about 45 minutes.

3. Add potatoes and simmer until meat and potatoes are tender. Add lemon juice and stir gently.

CAMBODIA

Location: Asia
Capital City: Phnom Penh
Language: Khmer, French
Monetary Unit: Riel

CAMBODIAN RICE
Servings: 4

Ingredients:

250	g	½	lb	lean pork, diced
2		2		chicken legs, diced
8		8		shrimp, shelled, deveined, diced
10		10		scallions, chopped
4		4		garlic cloves, minced
180	mL	¾	c	oil
750	mL	3	c	cooked rice
250	mL	1	c	medium white sauce
30	mL	2	T	vinegar
45	mL	3	T	brown sugar
				dash of fennel seed
				dash of Chinese five spice
				salt
				pepper
2		2		eggs, slightly beaten
1		1		pimento strips
30	mL	2	T	lemon juice

Method:

1. Beat eggs with salt and pepper and cook in a lightly oiled skillet. Do not stir. When eggs are cooked, remove from skillet and cut into very thin strips.

2. Heat oil in a large skillet and saute garlic and scallions. Add pork, chicken and shrimp and stir fry over medium-high heat for 20 minutes. Add rice, fennel seed, vinegar, white sauce, Chinese five spice, sugar, salt and pepper, one ingredient at a time. Keep stirring until well mixed. Stir in egg strips and sprinkle with lemon juice.

3. Serve garnished with pimento strips.

CAMEROON

Location:	Africa
Capital City:	Yaounde
Language:	French, English
Monetary Unit:	Franc CFA

COCONUT RICE
Servings: 6

Ingredients:

650	mL	2 ½ c	coconut milk (see page 71)
500	g	1 lb	stewing steak, cubed
500	mL	2 c	rice
2		2	large tomatoes, peeled, chopped
1		1	large onion, chopped
2		2	red chili, seeded, chopped
80	mL	⅓ c	tomato paste
60	mL	4 T	margarine
5	mL	1 t	thyme
			salt
			water

Method:

1. Saute onion and peppers in margarine until golden brown. Add tomatoes, tomato paste, thyme and salt. Simmer for 5 minutes and set aside.

2. Place meat in coconut milk, bring to a boil. Reduce heat and simmer for 30 minutes. Set aside.

3. Bring rice to a boil, strain. Add fresh water, boil again, then strain. Add rice to meat and coconut milk, then add onion and tomato mixture. Cook over low heat, stirring occasionally, until the rice absorb the coconut milk.

4. Garnish with diced hard boiled egg and tomatoes, and serve warm.

CANADA

Location: North America
Capital City: Ottawa
Language: English, French
Monetary Unit: Canadian Dollar

MAPLE SYRUP PIE
Servings: 6

Ingredients:

375	mL	1 ½ c	all-purpose flour
125	mL	½ c	shortening
60	mL	4 T	ice water
			pinch of salt
30	mL	2 T	butter
125	mL	½ c	brown sugar
250	mL	1 c	maple syrup
1		1	large egg, slightly beaten

Method:

1. Place flour and salt in a mixing bowl. Work in shortening with fingertips until mixture resembles coarse crumbs. Add water, a tablespoon at a time. Stir, using a fork, just until dough forms. Place on a floured surface and knead very lightly to form a smooth round ball. Wrap and refrigerate at least one hour.

2. Roll out pastry on lightly floured surface to a 23 cm (9 inch) circle and place it into a pie pan.

3. Cream butter and sugar together, add egg and maple syrup. Pour into pie pan on top of pie crust.

4. Bake in preheated oven at 250°C (450°F) for 15 minutes. Reduce heat to 180°C (350°F) and continue baking for 30 minutes or until the crust is golden.

5. Serve warm with vanilla ice cream on top.

CHAD

Location: Africa
Capital City: N'Djamena
Language: French, Arabic
Monetary Unit: Franc CFA

BEAN FRITTERS
Servings: 6

Ingredients:

250	mL	1	c	brown beans
1		1		onion, finely chopped
2	mL	½	t	ground red pepper
1		1		garlic clove, chopped
1		1		egg, beaten
5	mL	1	t	salt
				water
				oil for deep frying

Method:

1. Wash beans well and soak overnight. Drain and wash again. Place in saucepan, cover with fresh water and cook over medium heat for 1 hour or until beans are soft.

2. Remove the skins of the beans, discard skins. Puree beans with garlic and onion in an electric blender. Add salt, pepper, egg and a little water. Beat until light.

3. Shape the mixture into balls. Heat oil to 190°C (375°F) and fry fritters until golden.

4. Serve hot.

CHILE

Location: South America
Capital City: Santiago
Language: Spanish
Monetary Unit: Peso

PUMPKIN PATTIES
Servings: 4

Ingredients:

250	mL	1	c	cooked pumpkin
250	mL	1	c	flour
15	mL	1	T	baking powder
30	mL	2	T	butter
500	mL	2	c	oil
250	mL	1	c	honey or corn syrup
15	mL	1	T	corn starch
125	mL	½	c	water
				orange peels

Method:

1. Mix baking powder thoroughly with flour, then add pumpkin and butter. If necessary add more flour to make soft dough.

2. Roll with a rolling pin about 1.2 cm (½ inch) thick. Cut pieces with a round cookie cutter. Prick each pastry round with a fork to avoid puffing out.

3. Fry pastry pieces in very hot oil. Set aside.

4. Make a syrup with honey, orange peels and corn starch diluted in water. Boil ingredients together to make thick syrup.

5. Cover pumpkin patties with hot syrup and serve.

CHINA

Location: Asia
Capital City: Beijing
Language: Mandarin, Chinese, Yu
Monetary Unit: Yuan

FRIED EGG SHRIMP
Servings: 4

Ingredients:

500	g	1	lb	shrimp, frozen or fresh
750	mL	3	c	water
6		6		eggs
1		1		egg white
4		4		scallions, cut into pieces
60	mL	¼	c	peanut or salad oil
				salt
				black pepper

Method:

1. In boiling water, cook shrimp about 2 minutes. Set aside to cool.

2. Beat eggs with salt and black pepper. Add scallions.

3. In a bowl, combine shrimp with egg white.

4. Heat a wok very hot, then add oil and let it get quite hot. Fry shrimp in oil for 5 minutes. Pour in both egg mixtures. Stir constantly until cooked. (Do not let eggs get brown and crusty.)

5. Serve with rice.

COLOMBIA

Location:	South America
Capital City:	Bogota
Language:	Spanish
Monetary Unit:	Peso

MEAT AND VEGETABLE STEW
Servings: 6

Ingredients:

6		6		pieces of neck meat
250	g	½ lb		green beans
1		1		whole corn, cut in pieces
6		6		small potatoes
2		2		carrots, cut in pieces
1		1		chili pepper, seeded, sliced
125	mL	½ c		tomatoes, chopped
60	mL	¼ c		parsley, chopped
1		1		large onion, quartered
125	mL	½ c		cooked rice
				black pepper
				salt
45	mL	3	T	butter
500	mL	2	c	water

Method:

1. Fry meat in a saucepan, then add cold water. When water starts to boil, add salt, black pepper, parsley, onions, one carrot cut in pieces, tomatoes and chili pepper.

2. When meat is almost cooked, remove from saucepan and strain vegetable broth to give more richness and thickness. Return meat to broth and add remaining vegetables. Cook over medium low heat until everything is cooked.

3. Add rice 5 minutes before removing from heat.

COSTA RICA

Location:	Central America
Capital City:	San Jose
Language:	Spanish
Monetary Unit:	Colon

MEATBALL SOUP
Servings: 4

Ingredients:

500	g	1	lb	lean ground beef
1		1		egg
1		1		onion, grated
30	mL	2	T	parsley, finely chopped
				black pepper
				salt
125	mL	½	c	cornmeal
30	mL	2	T	oil
1		1		small onion, finely chopped
1		1		carrot, sliced
750	mL	3	c	beef broth

Method:

1. Mix meat, grated onion, egg and seasoning together. Form into small balls and roll in cornmeal. Set aside.

2. Melt butter in a saucepan, saute onion and carrots until onion is golden brown. Add beef broth and heat to a boil.

3. Add meat balls and bring to a boil again. Reduce heat and simmer until meatballs are done.

CUBA

Location:	Caribbean
Capital City:	Havana
Language:	Spanish
Monetary Unit:	Peso

CHICKEN AND RICE
Servings: 4

Ingredients:

1		1		medium chicken, quartered
2		2		garlic cloves, finely chopped
15	mL	1	T	lemon juice
1		1		large onion, finely chopped
125	mL	½	c	canned tomato
1		1		medium green pepper, chopped
1		1		medium pimento, chopped
125	mL	½	c	canned peas
125	mL	½	c	canned asparagus
5	mL	1	t	saffron
				salt
				black pepper
1		1		bay leaf
250	mL	1	c	dry wine
250	mL	1	c	chicken broth
250	mL	1	c	water
500	mL	2	c	rice
125	mL	½	c	oil

Method:

1. Heat oil, then add chicken and brown. Add onion, garlic, tomatoes, pimento, green pepper, asparagus, salt, black pepper, saffron, bay leaf, lemon juice, wine, broth and water. Bring to a boil. Remove bay leaf, reduce heat and cook about 30 minutes or until chicken is partially cooked.

2. Increase heat. When ingredients start boiling again, add rice and peas. Reduce heat to low, cook until rice is soft.

3. This recipe may be decorated with asparagus and hard boiled eggs.

CYPRUS

Location:	Asia
Capital City:	Nicosia
Language:	Greek, Turkish
Monetary Unit:	Cyprus Pound

OLIVE BREAD
Servings: 12

Ingredients:

750	mL	3	c	all purpose flour, sifted
3		3		eggs
180	mL	¾	c	olive oil
125	mL	½	c	yogurt
250	mL	1	c	black olives, pitted, chopped
5	mL	1	t	baking powder
5	mL	1	t	dried mint
30	mL	2	T	fresh lemon juice
				salt

Method:

1. Sift flour and baking powder together.

2. Beat together eggs, yogurt, oil, lemon juice, mint and salt. Add olives and combine with flour mixture.

3. Bake in a greased and floured loaf-pan at 180°C (350°F) in a preheated oven for 45 minutes or until the bread is golden brown and a skewer inserted into the centre of the loaf comes out clean.

4. Leave in pan for 5 minutes, then turn out onto a wire rack and cool. Serve sliced with butter.

CZECHOSLOVAKIA

Location:	Europe
Capital City:	Prague
Language:	Czech, Slovak
Monetary Unit:	Koruna

PRAGUE CAKE
Servings: 8

Ingredients:

100	g	3	oz	*semi-sweet chocolate*
90	mL	6	T	*unsalted butter*
180	mL	¾	c	*icing sugar*
4		4		*eggs*
180	mL	¾	c	*shredded almond*
60	mL	¼	c	*self rising pastry flour*
250	mL	1	c	*whipping cream*
30	mL	2	T	*cocoa*
15	mL	1	T	*sugar*
60	mL	¼	c	*apricot jam*

Method:

1. FOR CHOCOLATE WHIPPED CREAM: Mix cocoa and sugar with whipping cream. Bring to a boil. Set aside, let chill for at least 12 hours.

2. Grease and flour a 20 cm (8 inch) cake pan.

3. Melt chocolate over very low heat.

4. In a mixing bowl, cream butter with sugar. Add yolks and beat together. Add melted chocolate and almonds. Stir in beaten egg whites and flour.

5. Spread batter in cake pan and bake at 150°C (300°F) in a preheated oven for approximately 35 minutes.

6. Let cake cool. Spread apricot jam on top. Garnish with chocolate or plain whipped cream.

DENMARK

Location: Europe
Capital City: Copenhagen
Language: Danish
Monetary Unit: Krone

OPEN-FACED SANDWICHES
Basic Rules:

1. Use hearty, thinly sliced pumpernickel or French bread cut in half.

2. Cover the entire slice with butter so that moist topping will not soak though. Place a leaf of lettuce on one corner.

3. Use plenty of thin slices of topping, folding and overlapping so that none of the bread shows.

4. For a finishing touch, garnish with radish slices, tomato wedges, onion rings, cucumber twists or slices of fresh fruit, used in varying combinations.

Variations:

Danish Blue Cheese with Walnuts
Slice of Danish Blue Cheese, garnished with walnut halves.

Chicken Salad with Mushroom
Mound of chicken salad (mayonnaise seasoned with curry powder, salt and pepper to taste, mixed with cubes of cooked chicken, slices of fresh mushroom and asparagus spears), garnished with slices of fresh mushroom, slices of pepper and sprinkled with paprika.

Eggs with Danish
Slices of cooked eggs, garnished with mayonnaise and topped with Danish Caviar.

Havarti with Radishes
Slices of Danish Havarti cheese, garnished with sliced radishes, green and red pepper.

DENMARK (Continued)

Luncheon Meat with Cucumber
Slices of luncheon meat, garnished with thin slices of cucumber or chopped pickles.

Tongue with Horse Radish Salad
Thin tongue slices, garnished with creamed horse radish, wedge of tomato and spring of cress.

Cod's Roe with Remoulade
Slices of cod's roe, garnished with remoulade and cress.

DOMINICAN REPUBLIC

Location: Caribbean
Capital City: Santo Domingo
Language: Spanish
Monetary Unit: Peso

CHICKEN WITH PINEAPPLE
Servings: 6

Ingredients:

6		6	chicken legs
30	mL	2 T	lemon juice
			salt
			black pepper
			cayenne pepper
125	mL	1/2 c	peanut oil
1		1	large onion, finely chopped
1		1	garlic clove, chopped
1		1	green pepper, sliced
125	mL	1/2 c	canned tomato, chopped
125	mL	1/2 c	dry white wine
125	mL	1/2 c	chicken broth
250	mL	1 c	pineapple chunks, drained
60	mL	1/4 c	raisins
125	mL	1/2 c	split cashews
125	mL	1/2 c	amber rum
30	mL	2 T	corn starch

Method:

1. Rub chicken legs with lemon juice, season with salt, black pepper and cayenne. Set aside for 2-3 hours.

2. In a large pan, heat oil and lightly brown chicken legs. Add onion and garlic. Saute for 4 minutes. Add green pepper and tomatoes and cook 2-3 more minutes. Add wine and chicken broth. Cover and simmer over low heat for 20 minutes. Add cashews, raisins and pineapple, simmer about 15 minutes.

3. Remove chicken to a preheated platter. Keep warm.

4. Spoon off accumulated fat from sauce and discard. In a small bowl, mix rum with corn starch. Stir into sauce. Cook until thickened. Pour over chicken.

ECUADOR

Location: South America
Capital City: Quito
Language: Spanish, Quechua
Monetary Unit: Sucre

POTATO SOUP
Servings: 2

Ingredients:

1		1		medium onion, finely chopped
15	mL	1	T	butter
4		4		medium potatoes, cubed
950	mL	4	c	bouillon
125	mL	½	c	water
				paprika
				salt
125	mL	½	c	milk
15	mL	1	T	butter
30	mL	2	T	flour
1		1		egg yolk

Method:

1. In a saucepan, saute onion in 15 mL (1 T) butter until golden brown. Add water, potatoes and salt. Cook until potatoes are tender. Then blend potatoes and onion until it reaches the consistency of light cream. Add bouillon and keep warm.

2. In a pan, melt 15 mL (1 T) butter over low heat. Stir in flour, blend until smooth. Remove from heat, add beaten milk and yolk mixture gradually, stirring constantly until smooth and lump free.

3. Gradually add 250 mL (1 c) potato mixture to sauce. Then add this mixture to potato mixture. Stir constantly until boiled.

4. Garnish with paprika before serving.

EGYPT

Location:	Africa
Capital City:	Cairo
Language:	Arabic
Monetary Unit:	Egyptian Pound

BEAN SALAD
Servings: 4

Ingredients:

250	mL	1	c	navy beans
				water
				salt
2		2		garlic cloves, minced
60	mL	¼	c	oil
30	mL	2	T	lemon juice
3		3		scallions, sliced

Method:

1. Soak beans in water overnight. Drain and cover with fresh water. Cook until skins split. Drain well and cool.

2. Place beans in a bowl. Add salt, garlic, oil and lemon juice. Mix well. Chill in refrigerator.

3. Garnish with scallions before serving.

EL SALVADOR

Location: Central America
Capital City: San Salvador
Language: Spanish
Monetary Unit: Colon

MEAT AND VEGETABLE TORTILLAS
Servings: 8

Ingredients:

500	mL	2	c	cornmeal
500	mL	2	c	boiling water
				salt
250	mL	1	c	veal, cooked, diced
125	mL	½	c	potatoes, cooked, diced
125	mL	½	c	green pepper, chopped
60	mL	¼	c	red pepper, chopped
1		1		medium onion, sliced
1		1		medium tomato, chopped
15	mL	1	T	butter
				salt
				pepper
				oil for frying

Method:

1. TO MAKE TORTILLAS: Combine cornmeal and salt. Add boiling water and mix quickly until ingredients are combined. Divide dough into 8 equal portions and set aside for 20 minutes. Flatten each portion to about 13 cm (5 inch) diameter.

2. Saute the onion and peppers in butter until soft. Add veal and stir fry for 1 minute, then add tomato, potatoes, salt and pepper. Cook for another 2 minutes. Divide into 8 portions. Place each portion onto one half of each tortilla and spread evenly. Fold the other half of tortilla over and press edges together to seal.

3. Fry tortillas in hot shallow oil until each side is golden brown. Serve warm, with tomato and lettuce salad.

ETHIOPIA

Location: Africa
Capital City: Addis Ababa
Language: Amharic
Monetary Unit: Birr

HOT CHICKEN STEW
Servings: 4

Ingredients:

1		1	small chicken, cut up
80	mL	⅓ c	fresh lemon juice
1		1	small onion, grated
			salt
500	mL	2 c	water
60	mL	4 T	oil
4		4	medium onions, finely chopped
2		2	garlic cloves, finely chopped
5	mL	1 t	chili pepper
2	mL	½ t	black pepper
2	mL	½ t	ginger
2	mL	½ t	grounded coriander
2	mL	½ t	grounded cardamom
30	mL	2 T	tomato paste
			salt
60	mL	¼ c	dry white wine
4		4	hard boiled eggs, shelled

Method:

1. Rub chicken pieces with salt. Combine lemon juice, grated onion and 125 mL (½ c) water. Marinate chicken in this mixture at room temperature for an hour. Turn pieces several times.

2. Saute chopped onion in oil until transparent, then add garlic. Saute another 2 minutes. Add the rest of the water, chili powder, black pepper, ginger, coriander, cardamom, tomato paste and salt. Blend well. Bring to a boil, then reduce heat, cover and cook for 5 minutes. Add wine. Place marinated chicken pieces into sauce. Bring to a boil, then reduce heat, cover and simmer until chicken is tender.

3. Pierce each egg several times. Add them to sauce. Cover and cook 5 more minutes to permit sauce to penetrate eggs.

4. Serve hot with rice.

FINLAND

Location: Europe
Capital City: Helsinki
Language: Finnish, Swedish
Monetary Unit: Markka

SMELT CASSEROLE
Servings: 4

Ingredients:

500	g	1	lb		potatoes, peeled, sliced thinly
250	g	½ lb			smelt
30	mL	2	T		butter
					salt
					white pepper
1		1			onion, sliced thinly
6		6			sliced bacon, cut into medium pieces
1		1			egg
250	mL	1	c		milk

Method:

1. Grease an ovenproof glass dish with 15 mL (1 T) of butter. Cover bottom of dish with potato slices. Make a second layer with fish, sprinkle with salt and pepper, then add a layer of onion and bacon, then another layer of potatoes. Sprinkle with salt, pepper and bacon.

2. Beat egg with milk, pour over casserole. Dot with the rest of the butter.

3. Bake at 200°C (400°F) in a preheated oven about 1 hour.

FRANCE

Location: Europe
Capital City: Paris
Language: French
Monetary Unit: Franc

CHEESE SOUFFLE
Servings: 5

Ingredients:

60	mL	4	T	butter
4		4		eggs, separated
125	mL	½	c	flour
375	mL	1 ½	c	hot milk
180	mL	¾	c	grated cheese
				salt
				cayenne pepper
				nutmeg

Method:

1. Melt butter in a pan, add flour and cook slowly until flour just begins to turn golden brown.

2. Add milk and cook 5 minutes, mixing with a whip or slotted spoon. Add seasonings.

3. Beat yolks until light, then add a little of the hot mixture. When well combined, pour in the rest of the hot mixture. Reheat to boiling, stirring constantly. Remove from heat and add cheese.

4. Beat egg whites stiff, then fold them gently into cheese mixture.

5. Put into a greased souffle dish, filling only half way up.

6. Bake in a hot oven 225°C (425°F) about 20 minutes.

This souffle may be served with a flavoured cream sauce, if desired. Also a few spoonful of cooked spinach may be placed in the dish before the souffle mixture, or half a cup of lightly sauteed mushrooms.

GAMBIA

Location: Africa
Capital City: Banjul
Language: English
Monetary Unit: Dalasi

LAMB AND CHICKEN RICE
Servings: 6

Ingredients:

½ kg	1	lb	lamb shoulder, cubed
½ kg	1	lb	chicken breast, cubed
125 mL	½	c	fresh lemon juice
75 mL	5	T	peanut oil
1	1		Spanish onion, chopped
	4		tomatoes, chopped
5 mL	1	t	ginger
2 mL	½	t	thyme
1	1		bay leaf
15 mL	1	T	fresh chili pepper, chopped
			salt
			black pepper
500 mL	2	c	rice
500 mL	2	c	water

Method:

1. Marinate lamb and chicken in lemon juice in refrigerator overnight. Remove meat, patting dry. Reserve marinate.

2. In a pan, heat oil and brown meat. Transfer meat and keep warm. In same oil saute onions until golden brown. Stir in tomatoes, ginger, thyme, bay leaf, chili peppers, salt, black pepper, water and marinate.

3. Return lamb to pan. Cover and simmer for 25 minutes. Stir in chicken, simmer another 10 minutes.

4. Add washed rice. Cover and simmer for 25 minutes, stirring once, over very low heat.

5. Discard bay leaf and serve immediately.

GERMANY

Location: Europe
Capital City: Berlin
Language: German
Monetary Unit: Deutsche Mark

POTATO SALAD
Servings: 6

Ingredients:

1	kg	2 lb		potatoes
125	mL	½ c		mayonnaise
1		1		large onion, diced
1		1		apple, diced
3		3		pickled cucumbers, diced
3		3		tomatoes, diced
				vinegar
				pepper
				sugar
				salt
125	mL	½ c		hot bouillon

Method:

1. Boil potatoes in skins and leave to cool. Remove skins and cut potatoes into thin slices.

2. Place potatoes in a salad bowl and add onion, apple, cucumber, and tomato. Mix in mayonnaise and add pepper, salt, sugar and vinegar to taste.

3. Pour over hot bouillon and mix well. Leave to stand for at least 1 hour before serving.

GERMANY (Continued)

BEEF ROLL
Servings: 4

Ingredients:

4		4		slices of shoulder beef
20	mL	4	t	continental mustard
2		2		onions, sliced
4		4		slices of lean bacon
2		2		dill pickles, cut into halves
				salt
				pepper
500	mL	2	c	hot water
5	mL	1	t	corn starch
60	mL	¼	c	oil

Method:

1. Beat each slice of meat. Spread each with mustard, cover with onion and lay a strip of bacon down the centre of each slice. Place a pickle across the narrow end of each piece and roll meat around it. Fasten with skewers or twine.

2. Sear rolls in hot oil, brown evenly on all sides. Remove from skillet. Add hot water slowly to skillet, loosen all brown meat particles from bottom of pan. Return rolls to skillet. Cover and simmer for 1 hour or until meat is tender.

3. Thicken sauce with corn starch.

4. Serve with mashed potatoes or noodles.

GHANA

Location: Africa
Capital City: Accra
Language: English
Monetary Unit: Cedi

SPINACH STEW
Servings: 6

Ingredients:

900	g	2	lb	spinach
4		4		tomatoes, finely chopped
450	g	1	lb	meat, cut into pieces
450	g	1	lb	smoked fish, cut into pieces
1		1		large onion, finely chopped
125	mL	½	c	ground pumpkin seeds
				few smoked shrimp, chopped
				salt
				pepper
180	mL	¾	c	palm or corn oil
				water

Method:

1. Put meat into a saucepan, sprinkle with salt, add onions and water to cover. Let this boil until water evaporates. Add a little water and simmer until meat is tender. Set aside.

2. Pick over and wash spinach and cook in 500 mL (2 c) water for 5 minutes. Strain and chop spinach and save cooking liquid.

3. Mix ground pumpkin seeds with a little water.

4. In a pan, heat oil and fry tomatoes and shrimp. Add seed mixture, fish, spinach, meat and spinach liquid. Add salt and pepper. Simmer for 40 minutes or fish is tender. Stir occasionally.

5. Serve hot with rice.

GREECE

Location:	Europe
Capital City:	Athens
Language:	Greek
Monetary Unit:	Drachma

FISH ROE DIP
Servings: 2

Ingredients:

75	mL	5	T	carp roe
1		1		small onion, finely grated
180	mL	¾	c	olive or corn oil
5		5		slices white bread, crumbed
2		2		lemons

Method:

1. Mash carp roe and add onion. Add a little oil and beat thoroughly to a smooth paste.

2. Add alternately bread, oil and lemon juice. Beat until cream coloured.

3. Serve as a dip with crackers or spread on toast.

GUADELOUPE

Location:	Caribbean
Capital City:	Basse-Terre
Language:	French
Monetary Unit:	Franc

HAM ROLLS
Servings: 4

Ingredients:

15	mL	1 T	butter
20	mL	4 t	flour
180	mL	¾ c	beef broth
			salt
			white pepper
60	mL	¼ c	whipping cream
30	mL	2 T	dark rum
4		4	slices of ham
180	mL	¾ c	spinach, cooked and chopped
7	mL	½ T	butter
2	mL	½ t	flour
60	mL	¼ c	milk

Method:

1. Melt butter, stir in flour, mix well. Gradually add beef broth, stirring constantly. Boil until sauce is thick and reduced to half its original volume. Season with salt and pepper. Reduce heat, then add cream.

2. Add rum to sauce. Add ham slices, heat thoroughly.

3. In a pan, melt butter and stir in flour. Add milk and cook 2 minutes, stirring constantly. Add warm spinach, stir well. Divide into 4 portions.

4. Transfer ham slices from sauce. Place spinach mixture on each slice then roll up. Transfer to a baking dish, pour sauce over ham rolls and broil about 5 minutes.

GUATEMALA

Location: Central America
Capital City: Guatemala City
Language: Spanish, Indian Dialects
Monetary Unit: Quetzal

AVOCADO SALAD
Servings: 6

Ingredients:

2		2	avocados, diced
2		2	eggs, hard boiled, diced
2		2	medium tomatoes, diced
1		1	small onion, minced
4		4	stuffed green olives, sliced
30	mL	2 T	oil
1		1	lemon
			chili powder

Method:

1. Gently mix the first five ingredients.

2. Add oil and lemon juice. Sprinkle with chili powder.

GUINEA

Location:	Africa
Capital City:	Conakry
Language:	French
Monetary Unit:	Guinean Franc

CHICKEN WITH OKRA
Servings: 4

Ingredients:

4		*4*	*small chicken legs*
30	*mL*	*2 T*	*lemon juice*
			salt
45	*mL*	*3 T*	*peanut oil*
1		*1*	*large onion, finely chopped*
125	*mL*	*½ c*	*canned tomato, chopped*
125	*mL*	*½ c*	*chicken broth*
250	*g*	*½ lb*	*okra*
15	*mL*	*1 T*	*lemon juice*
125	*mL*	*½ c*	*peanut butter*
60	*mL*	*¼ c*	*water*

Method:

1. Rub chicken legs with 30 mL (2 T) lemon juice, sprinkle with salt, and set aside for an hour.

2. In a large pan, heat oil and lightly brown chicken. Remove to a casserole pan, cover and keep warm. Add onion to oil and saute for 4 minutes. Add tomatoes, chicken broth, lemon juice and okra. Stir gently and cook for 5 minutes, then pour over chicken.

3. Smooth peanut butter with water and pour over chicken. Cover and cook in a preheated 180°C (350°F) oven for an hour.

4. Serve hot with rice pilaff.

GUYANA

Location: South America
Capital City: Georgetown
Language: English
Monetary Unit: Guyana Dollar

CURRIED FISH
Servings: 2

Ingredients:

450	g	1	lb	fish fillet
				salt
				black pepper
				cayenne pepper
				oil for frying
1		1		small onion, finely chopped
30	mL	2	T	butter
5	mL	1	t	curry powder
180	mL	¾	c	coconut milk (see page 71)
				lemon rings

Method:

1. Season fish fillets with salt, pepper and cayenne for about 20 minutes.

2. Fry fish on both sides until light brown in colour. Set aside.

3. In a pan, heat butter and fry onion lightly for a few minutes. Mix curry powder to paste with a little water and stir in with onion.

4. Add fish and cook for a few minutes. Then add coconut milk and simmer gently for about 20 minutes. Do not allow fish break down.

5. Remove fish to a hot dish. Pour gravy around fish and decorate with lemon rings.

HAITI

Location:	Caribbean
Capital City:	Port-au-Prince
Language:	French, Creole
Monetary Unit:	Gourde

SWEET POTATO CAKE
Servings: 6

Ingredients:

250	mL	1	c	sweet potato, mashed
2		2		bananas, mashed
250	mL	1	c	milk
60	mL	¼	c	sugar
60	mL	¼	c	seedless raisins
3		3		eggs, beaten
1	mL	¼	t	allspice
1	mL	¼	t	cinnamon
1	mL	¼	t	salt

Method:

1. Combine sweet potato and bananas. Add milk and blend; then add sugar, allspice, cinnamon, eggs and raisins. Mix well.

2. Pour into a well greased loaf pan. Bake at 180°C (350°F) in a preheated oven for 1 hour or until firm and golden brown on top.

3. Let cool, then place on serving dish.

HONDURAS

Location:	Central America
Capital City:	Tegucigalpa
Language:	Spanish
Monetary Unit:	Lemripa

HONDURAS STYLE CHICKEN
Servings: 4

Ingredients:

1		*1*	*medium chicken, cut up*
2		*2*	*garlic cloves, minced*
60	*mL*	*4 T*	*oil*
4		*4*	*tomatoes, peeled, chopped*
2		*2*	*large pimentos, sliced*
14		*14*	*stuffed olives, sliced*
125	*mL*	*½ c*	*tomato juice*
			salt
			pepper

Method:

1. Brown garlic in hot oil. Add chicken pieces and brown on all sides.

2. Add tomatoes, pimentos, olives, salt, pepper and tomato juice. Cover and simmer over low heat for 90 minutes or until tender.

3. Serve with rice.

HUNGARY

Location:	Europe
Capital City:	Budapest
Language:	Magray
Monetary Unit:	Forint

GOULASH
Servings: 4

Ingredients:

600	g	1 ¼ lb		stewing beef
60	mL	4	T	butter
4		4		medium onions, finely chopped
2		2		garlic cloves, crushed
15	mL	1	T	paprika
				salt
				caraway seeds
				black pepper
3		3		green peppers, coarsely chopped
4		4		tomatoes, peeled, chopped
700	g	2	lb	potatoes, cubed largely
1		1		egg
250	mL	1	c	flour

Method:

1. Brown beef in a little oil in a large skillet. Transfer beef to a Dutch oven. Rinse the skillet with 250 mL (1 c) water and add resulting liquid to meat. Cover and cook slowly over low heat.

2. Fry onions in remaining oil. Stir in paprika, salt, caraway seeds, black pepper and garlic, then combine with simmering meat.

3. When meat is partially cooked, add potatoes, green pepper and tomatoes. Continue cooking slowly until meat is tender. Be careful not to overcook potatoes.

4. In the meantime, make a stiff dough with egg and flour. Roll out and cut into strips. Add to goulash and cook until soft.

5. Serve hot.

ICELAND

Location: Europe
Capital City: Reykjavik
Language: Icelandic
Monetary Unit: M.N. Krona

HERRING SALAD
Servings: 4

Ingredients:

450	g	16	oz	jar herring, sliced
130	g	8	oz	jar pickled beets
1		1		apple
1		1		large boiled potato, cold
1		1		small onion
15	mL	1	T	prepared mustard
30	mL	2	T	mayonnaise
2		2		eggs, hard boiled
5	mL	1	t	sugar
				pepper
15	mL	1	T	juice from the beet jar
5	mL	1	t	vinegar

Method:

1. Cut herring, beet, apple, potato and onion into small pieces and mix together in a bowl.

2. Add mustard, mayonnaise, sugar, pepper, beet juice and vinegar. Mix well and chill for ½ hour.

3. Garnish with chopped hard boiled eggs, before serving. Will keep for weeks in refrigerator.

INDIA

Location: Asia
Capital City: New Delhi
Language: Hindi, English
Monetary Unit: Rupee

EGG AND MUSHROOM CURRY
Servings: 4

Ingredients:

6		6	eggs, hard boiled
250	g	½ lb	small white mushroom
15	mL	1 T	butter
5	mL	1 t	ginger, finely chopped
10	mL	2 t	salt
10	mL	2 t	garam masala
30	mL	⅛ c	yogurt
3		3	medium tomatoes, sliced
1		1	medium onion, finely chopped
30	mL	2 T	parsley, chopped
2	mL	½ t	turmeric
2	mL	½ t	chili powder
7	mL	½ T	lemon juice

Method:

1. Fry onion and ginger in butter. Add turmeric, parsley, garam masala and chili powder. Then add tomatoes and yogurt. Turn heat slightly higher to dry off excess liquid.

2. Add mushrooms, mix and fry for several minutes, then cover saucepan and cook on medium heat for 15 minutes.

3. Shell eggs and cut in half slantwise. Carefully place them in curry sauce. Shake saucepan so that eggs are well coated in sauce.

4. Uncover and cook for 15 minutes, shaking saucepan frequently. (If extra juicy curry is required, the lid should be kept on.)

5. Add lemon juice, mix well, then curry is ready to serve.

INDONESIA

Location:	Asia
Capital City:	Jakarta
Language:	Bahasa Indonesia,
Monetary Unit:	Rupiah

FRIED RICE
Servings: 4

Ingredients:

500	mL	2	c	uncooked rice
125	g	¼	lb	raw shrimp, shelled, deveined
250	g	½	lb	lean beef, cut into thin strips
1		1		medium onion, grated
1		1		garlic clove, minced
4		4		scallions, snipped
3		3		eggs, beaten
30	mL	2	T	soy sauce
				salt
				black pepper
90	mL	6	T	oil

Method:

1. Cook rice in plenty of boiling salted water until just tender. Drain and rinse with cold water.

2. In a pan, heat 30 mL (2 T) oil and saute the beef until tender, turning frequently. Remove from pan. Saute shrimp in same manner.

3. To same pan add 30mL (2 T) oil and saute garlic, onion and scallions until golden brown. Add beaten eggs, salt and pepper. Cook, stirring, until just set (do not let dry). Remove mixture from pan.

4. To the same pan add 30 mL (2 T) oil, add rice and heat through. Add shrimp, beef, egg mixture and soy sauce. Blend well.

IRAN

Location: Asia
Capital City: Teheran
Language: Farsi, Arabic, Turkish
Monetary Unit: Rial

FILAFEL
Servings: 6

Ingredients:

500	mL	2	c	dry split fava beans
1		1		small bunch parsley
1		1		bunch scallions
15	mL	1	T	red pepper
15	mL	1	T	black pepper
30	mL	2	T	salt
60	mL	4	T	coriander
30	mL	2	T	ground cumin
45	mL	3	T	dill weed
6		6		garlic cloves
3		3		medium onions, chopped
45	mL	3	T	sesame seeds
				flour
				baking powder
				water
				oil for deep frying
				Tahini dressing

Method:

1. Cover fava beans in water and soak for 24 hours. Drain well.

2. Grind beans, parsley, scallions, onions, red pepper, black pepper, salt, coriander, cumin, dill weed and garlic. Mix very well.

3. Measure ground ingredients. For each cup add 30 mL (2 T) flour. Then add sesame seeds. (At this point, unused portion of the batter may be frozen.)

4. At frying time, for each cup of batter add 2.5 mL (½ t) of baking powder and mix well. For each cup of filling, add 15 mL (1 T) of water to make a smooth but thick batter.

5. Drop batter, one dessert spoon at a time, into 180°C (350°F) oil. Turn occasionally until the Filafel is lightly browned. Drain on paper towels.

6. Serve tahini dressing on Filafel. Also serve with green salad.

IRAN (Continued)

TAHINI DRESSING

60	mL	4	T	sesame tahini
60	mL	4	T	water
30	mL	2	T	white vinegar
5	mL	1	t	salt
5	mL	1	t	black pepper
5	mL	1	t	ground cumin
2	mL	½	t	allspice

Mix all the above ingredients very well and spoon over Filafel.
Yields enough for 4 servings.

GREEN SALAD

1	medium tomato, diced
½	cucumber, diced
6	leaves lettuce, shredded
1	small onion, diced
	oil
	lemon juice
	salt
	pepper

IRAQ

Location: Asia
Capital City: Baghdad
Language: Arabic
Monetary Unit: Iraqi Dinar

IRAQI KEBABS
Servings: 10

Ingredients:

450	g	1	lb	lamb ground
450	g	1	lb	lean beef ground
1		1		egg white, beaten
1		1		large onion, minced
5	mL	1	t	salt
5	mL	1	t	paprika
2		2		large onion, finely chopped
4		4		garlic cloves, minced
30	mL	2	T	oil

Method:

1. Fry chopped onion and garlic in oil until well cooked.

2. Place meat, fried onion and garlic, minced onion, salt, paprika and egg white in a large bowl and mix well.

3. Thread mixture onto skewers and chill about 4 to 6 hours.

4. Grill 12 cm (4 inch) above charcoal, turning once, about 8 minutes on each side.

5. Serve hot with rice or bulgur pilaff.

IRELAND

Location:	Europe
Capital City:	Dublin
Language:	Irish, English
Monetary Unit:	Irish Pound

DUBLIN CODDLE
Servings: 8

Ingredients:

8		8		thick slices back bacon
500	g	1	lb	pork sausages
4		4		large onions, sliced
8		8		large potatoes, peeled, sliced
900	mL	4	c	water
				parsley, chopped
				salt
				pepper

Method:

1. Boil sausages and bacon in 900 mL (4 c) water for five minutes. Remove meat and reserve liquid.

2. Place all ingredients in a fireproof dish. Season to taste. Add enough liquid to cover. Cover with lid and simmer gently about 1 hour or until the ingredients form a semi-thick stew.

IRISH COFFEE
Servings: 1

Ingredients:

1		1		double Irish whisky
15	mL	1	T	double cream, cold
250	mL	1	c	black coffee, strong, hot
7	mL	½	T	sugar

Method:

1. Warm a whisky glass, add sugar and enough coffee to dissolve sugar. Add whisky. Hold a teaspoon curved side up across the glass and poor the cream slowly over the spoon. The hot whisky-laced coffee is drunk through the cold cream which is floating on top of the coffee.

ISRAEL

Location: Asia
Capital City: Jerusalem
Language: Hebrew, Arabic
Monetary Unit: Shekel

BULGUR WHEAT SALAD
Servings: 6

Ingredients:

375	mL	1 ½ c	raw bulgur wheat
1	L	4 c	boiling water
250	mL	1 c	parsley, finely chopped
180	mL	¾ c	fresh mint, finely chopped
180	mL	¾ c	scallions, finely chopped
3		3	medium tomatoes, chopped
180	mL	¾ c	lemon juice
60	mL	¼ c	oil
			salt
			black pepper

Method:

1. Pour boiling water over bulgur. Cover and let stand for 2 hours. Drain excess water and press out remaining water.

2. Mix in remaining ingredients. Chill at least one hour (the longer it stands the better it is).

3. It can also be served in pita as a sandwich.

ITALY

Location: Europe
Capital City: Rome
Language: Italian
Monetary Unit: Lira

ITALIAN VEAL STEW
Servings: 6

Ingredients:

6		6	veal shank cross cuts
60	mL	1/4 c	flour
			pepper
60	mL	1/4 c	butter
60	mL	1/4 c	oil
125	mL	1/2 c	onion, chopped
2		2	garlic cloves, crushed
1		1	carrot, sliced
1		1	celery stalk, sliced
			sage
			rosemary
			salt
30	mL	2 T	tomato paste
250	mL	1 c	dry red wine
500	mL	2 c	water
5		5	pieces anchovies, cut into pieces
1		1	lemon
			parsley, chopped

Method:

1. Dredge meat with salted flour; brown in oil and butter mixture. Transfer to a pot.

2. To the same fat add onion, garlic, carrot and celery. Fry until onion is golden brown. Add seasonings, tomato paste, wine and water. Bring to a boil; reduce heat and cover pot. Simmer 2 hours or until meat is tender.

3. Remove meat gently from pot. Place liquid in a blender and make a smooth sauce. Pour sauce over meat and keep hot. Shortly before serving add anchovies, thin slivers of lemon and parsley.

IVORY COST

Location: Africa
Capital City: Yamoussoukro
Language: French, African Languages
Monetary Unit: Frank CFA

BANANA FRITTERS
Servings: 6

Ingredients:

375	mL	1 ½ c	milk
1		1	egg
30	mL	2 T	sugar
180	mL	¾ c	flour
2		2	large bananas
5	mL	1 t	baking powder
			pinch of nutmeg
			oil for deep frying

Method:

1. Peel and mash bananas till smooth.

2. Mix flour with baking powder and nutmeg.

3. Beat sugar with egg until light; add milk. To this mixture add mashed bananas and flour. Mix all together to form a medium soft consistency.

4. Heat oil to 190°C (375°F) and drop in beaten banana mixture by the heaping tablespoon and fry. If desired sprinkle with icing sugar before serving.

JAMAICA

Location:	Caribbeans
Captial City:	Kingston
Language:	English, Creole
Monetary Unit:	Jamaican Dollar

JAMAICAN RICE
Servings: 4

Ingredients:

250	g	½ lb		stewing pork, cubed
250	g	½ lb		stewing beef, cubed
45	mL	3	T	bacon drippings or peanut oil
30	mL	2	T	flour
5	mL	1	t	seasoned salt
1		1		medium onion, finely chopped
2		2		medium tomatoes, chopped
1		1		medium eggplant, cubed
1		1		medium carrot, chopped
250	mL	1	c	cabbage, shredded
250	mL	1	c	converted rice
500	mL	2	c	beef bouillon
250	mL	1	c	water

Method:

1. Put flour and seasoned salt in a paper bag, add meat and coat well.

2. In a Dutch oven, brown meat on all sides, add onion, eggplant and carrots. Cook all together over moderate heat for 10 minutes, stirring frequently. Add tomatoes, cabbage, bouillon, water and salt. Bring to a boil, then add rice. Again bring to a boil, then lower heat and simmer covered for 40 minutes or until tender.

3. Stir gently and serve warm.

JAPAN

Location:	Asia
Captial City:	Tokyo
Language:	Japanese
Monetary Unit:	Yen

BATTER FRIED SHRIMP AND VEGETABLES
Servings: 4

Ingredients:

8		8	jumbo shrimp
8		8	mushroom, whole
12		12	green beans, trimmed
1		1	carrot, cut in strips
1		1	sweet potato, peeled, cut in slices
60	mL	¼ c	mirin or rice wine or sherry
60	mL	¼ c	soy sauce
250	mL	1 c	water or fish stock
80	mL	⅓ c	white radish, grated
15	mL	1 T	ginger, grated
2		2	eggs
500	mL	2 c	flour
160	mL	⅔ c	water, for vegetable batter
180	mL	¾ c	water, for shrimp batter

Method:

1. FOR DIPPING SAUCE: Combine mirin, soy sauce and 250 mL (1 c) water or fish stock in a pan and bring to a boil. Remove from heat and let cool.

2. FOR BOTH BATTERS: Beat 1 egg slightly with cold water (use correct amount of water for each type of batter). Sift 250 mL (1 c) flour over each egg mixture and stir slightly.

3. Remove shrimp shells, leaving last segment and tail on.

4. Wash all vegetables, pat dry.

5. Dip ingredients in the correct batter. Deep fry vegetables first, then shrimp at 180°C (350°F), turning once. Drain on paper towels. Keep warm.

6. Pour dipping sauce into individual bowls. Add radish and ginger to sauce and mix. Place two of shrimp, mushrooms and vegetables on a serving dish with sauce bowl.

JORDAN

Location: Asia
Captial City: Amman
Language: Arabic, English
Monetary Unit: Jordanian Dinar

ARTICHOKE CASSEROLE
Servings: 4

Ingredients:

15		15	artichoke hearts, canned
375	mL	1 ½ c	yogurt
250	mL	1 c	water
15	mL	1 T	cornstarch
1		1	egg
15	mL	1 T	tahini
			juice of one-half lemon
3		3	garlic cloves
5	mL	1 t	dried coriander
500	g	1 lb	ground beef
1		1	onion, finely chopped
60	mL	¼ c	pine nuts
15	mL	1 T	butter
			salt
			pepper
			allspice

Method:

1. Saute onions with meat, salt, pepper and allspice; remove from pan. In the same butter, saute pine nuts until lightly brown; remove from pan. Saute 2 garlic cloves and coriander; remove from pan. Keep them separately.

2. Mince one garlic clove, add tahini and lemon juice.

3. Mix yogurt with 125 mL (½ c) water, add well beaten egg, garlic and tahini sauce, and the cornstarch diluted in a little cold water. Beat well. Place the saucepan on low heat, bring to a boil, stirring constantly. When boiling, reduce heat as much as possible to prevent yogurt from curdling. Simmer uncovered for 5 minutes.

4. In a large fireproof dish, place artichokes and fill them with meat mixture. Pour yogurt sauce over atrichokes, and dot with pine nuts. Garnish the dish with sauteed coriander and garlic.

5. Bake in 180°C (350°F) oven for 30 minutes.

KENYA

Location:	Africa
Captial City:	Nairobi
Language:	Swahili, English
Monetary Unit:	Kenyan Shilling

GREEN MASHED POTATO
Servings: 6

Ingredients:

250	mL	1	c	whole kernel corn, boiled
250	mL	1	c	white beans, boiled
250	mL	1	c	peas, boiled
6		6		medium potatoes, boiled
45	mL	3	T	butter
				salt

Method:

1. Mash hot potatoes and peas together. Add butter and salt and mix well.

2. Stir in beans and corn, mix gently. Keep warm and serve with any kind of steak.

KOREA, REPUBLIC OF

Location:	Asia
Captial City:	Seoul
Language:	Korean
Monetary Unit:	Won

BEEF WITH VEGETABLES
Servings: 8

Ingredients:

1		1		small bag of bean thread
500	g	1	lb	lean and tender beef
3		3		large carrots, peeled, threaded
2		2		large onions, sliced
2		2		large green pepper, sliced thinly
2		2		roots of scallions, sliced thinly
5		5		large mushrooms, sliced
3		3		large Chinese dried mushrooms
15	mL	1	T	soy sauce
1	mL	¼	t	sesame oil
2	mL	½	t	sugar
				black pepper
				garlic powder
				peanut oil for sauteeing vegetables

Method:

1. Soak dried mushrooms in hot water for half an hour or until they become soft. Slice into small pieces.

2. Cook bean thread in boiling water as you would cook spaghetti. Drain, lay out on a cutting board and cut in two or three places. Set aside.

3. Saute vegetables one at a time in a large wok with 2 mL (½ t) peanut oil for each vegetable. (The best way of sauteeing vegetables is to put oil in the wok and sprinkle with salt. When wok becomes hot put vegetables in at once and stir quickly for a few minutes on high heat.) Put all sauteed vegetables in a large bowl.

4. Saute beef with a sprinkle of garlic powder, sugar and 2 mL (½ t) of soy sauce. Remove from wok and put with vegetables. Add sesame oil, black pepper, remaining sugar, bean thread and soy sauce to the cooked beef and vegetables. Mix together well. Add soy sauce, sugar or black pepper to taste.

5. Serve warm.

KUWAIT

Location:	Asia
Captial City:	Kuwait
Language:	Arabic, English
Monetary Unit:	Kuwaiti Dinar

KUWAITI DESSERT
Servings: 8

Ingredients:

500	mL	2	c	gram flour
250	mL	1	c	unbleached flour
10	mL	2	t	corn starch
10	mL	2	t	yeast
400	mL	1 ½	c	yogurt
1		1		boiled potato, mashed
				oil for deep frying
500	mL	2	c	water
500	mL	2	c	sugar
15	mL	1	T	fresh lemon juice
60	mL	¼ c		rose water
				pinch of saffron

Method:

1. Boil water, sugar and the lemon. Add saffron and rose water. Let cool.

2. Combine gram flour, unbleached flour and corn starch. Mix with yogurt. Add yeast, then make dough. Let stand for 2 hours or until it rises.

3. Push dough down. Add mashed potato and mix well.

4. Wet hands and press dough into small balls. Deep fry in oil. Place balls in a dry pan and add syrup.

LAOS

Location: Asia
Captial City: Vientiane
Language: Lao, French
Monetary Unit: Kip

CHICKEN WITH COCONUT MILK
Servings: 4

Ingredients:

1		1	medium whole chicken
750	mL	3 c	flaked coconut
250	mL	1 c	hot water
750	mL	3 c	hot water
125	mL	½ c	peanuts
500	mL	2 c	raw grounded pork
2		2	small onions, chopped and fried
4		4	grilled pimentos, chopped
			fennel
			cinnamon
			mint
			salt
			black pepper

Method:

1. To make the coconut milk, pour 500 mL (2 c) hot water over flaked coconut. Allow to soak for 15 minutes. Strain through a fine sieve. This will give you the first coconut milk. Measure out 250 mL (1 c) and set aside. Pour 500 mL (2 c) of hot water over coconut again with the rest of the first milk. Allow to soak 15 minutes. Strain. Measure 750-1000 mL (3-4 c) of second coconut milk.

2. Prepare the stuffing by pounding peanuts, pork, onion, pimento and seasoning. Bind stuffing with first coconut milk (250 mL which you reserved).

3. Introduce stuffing in well cleaned chicken. Secure cavity opening and place in a saucepan.

4. Pour second coconut milk over chicken. Sprinkle with salt. Cook over low heat with lid on until coconut milk is reduced to a cream.

LEBANON

Location:	Asia
Captial City:	Beirut
Language:	Arabic, English, French
Monetary Unit:	Lebanese Pound

LEBANESE BREAD-PITA

Servings: 8

Ingredients:

750	mL	3	c	unbleached flour
15	mL	1	T	yeast
250	mL	1	c	warm water
5	mL	1	t	sugar
				salt
				water
				cornmeal

Method:

1. Dissolve the sugar in warm water. Sprinkle yeast over warm water and leave in a warm place for 10 minutes or until frothy.

2. In a large bowl, sieve together flour and salt. Pour in yeast and water mixture, and add enough water to make a soft dough.

3. Place dough on a floured surface and knead for about 10 minutes or until dough is smooth and elastic. Put in a oiled bowl covered with a damp cloth and set in a warm place for 2 hours.

4. Punch dough down and knead lightly. Divide into 8 portions. Let rest 1 hour at room temperature. Roll out each piece until it is 5 mm (¼ inch) thick. Cut 8 squares of foil. Sprinkle each piece of foil with cornmeal and place the flat dough. Place them in oven.

5. Bake in 260°C (500°F) in a preheated oven for 6 minutes. Remove and allow to cool.

LESOTHO

Location:	Africa
Captial City:	Maseru
Language:	Sesotho, English
Monetary Unit:	Loti

BEAN MILLET PUMPKIN STEW
Servings: 4

Ingredients:

500	mL	2	c	cooked beans
250	mL	1	c	cooked millet
250	mL	1	c	cooked pumpkin
15	mL	1	T	butter
5	mL	1	t	salt
125	mL	½	c	onion, chopped
15	mL	1	T	oil
				black pepper
				cinnamon (optional)

Method:

1. Fry the onion in oil until tender. Add millet, salt, pepper and beans. Cook over low heat, stirring constantly, until the mixture is thick.

2. Stir in pumpkin and butter. The mixture will be quite thick after about 15 minutes. Serve as a main dish.

Variation:

This can also be made into small balls when cold and deep fried. (Coat the balls with flour.)

LIBERIA

Location: Africa
Captial City: Monrovia
Language: English
Monetary Unit: Liberian Dollar

LIBERIAN RICE
Servings: 6

Ingredients:

6	6	chicken thighs
80 mL	1/3 c	oil
180 mL	3/4 c	cooked ham, diced
2	2	medium onion, sliced
2	2	large tomatoes, chopped
125 mL	1/2 c	cabbage, shredded
		salt
		black pepper
750 mL	3 c	water
375 mL	1 1/2 c	rice

Method:

1. Rub the chicken thighs with salt and pepper then fry them in heated oil until golden brown on all sides. Remove and place chicken in a Dutch oven.

2. Fry ham in same oil. Remove ham from oil and add to chicken, along with onions, tomatoes, cabbage and water. Bring to a boil. Reduce heat to low, cover and simmer until chicken is tender.

3. Remove chicken from Dutch oven. Bring mixture to a boil. Add rice, reduce heat, cover and cook until rice is almost done. Then add chicken pieces again, cook another 5 minutes. (If necessary add more water.)

4. Serve warm.

LIBYA

Location: Africa
Captial City: Tripoli
Language: Arabic
Monetary Unit: Libyan Dinar

CHICKEN DISH
Servings: 6

Ingredients:

4		*4*		*boneless chicken breast, cubed*
1		*1*		*large onion, finely chopped*
1		*1*		*large green pepper, chopped*
1		*1*		*large tomatoes, chopped*
225	*g*	*8*	*oz*	*mushrooms, sliced*
125	*mL*	*½*	*c*	*water*
65	*mL*	*3*	*T*	*butter*
				salt
				paprika

Method:

1. Saute onions, mushrooms and pepper in butter. Add tomatoes and water. Simmer for 2 minutes.

2. Add the chicken breast. Season with salt and paprika. Cook about 10 minutes or until meat is cooked.

3. Serve hot with rice pilaff.

LUXEMBOURG

Location:	Europe
Captial City:	Luxembourg
Language:	French, German
Monetary Unit:	Luxembourg Franc

LIVER DUMPLINGS
Servings: 4

Ingredients:

450	g	1	lb	beef liver
1		1		large onion
1		1		leek, white parts, minced
1		1		egg
30	mL	⅛	c	parsley, finely chopped
125	mL	½	c	fresh bread crumbs
5	mL	1	t	brandy
5		5		slices of bacon
				salt
				black pepper

Method:

1. Grind raw liver, onion and leek. Add bread crumbs, egg, parsley, salt, pepper and brandy. Mix well.

2. Meanwhile bring 1.5 L (6 c) of water to a boil. Drop a meat mixture, one tablespoonful at a time, into boiling water. Cover pan and simmer for 10 minutes. (Dip tablespoon in hot water each time before scooping.)

3. Cut bacon in small pieces and fry until golden brown. Pour bacon and fat over dumplings placed on heated plate.

4. Serve warm with baked or boiled potatoes.

MADEIRA

Location:	Atlantic Ocean
Port City:	Punchal
Language:	Portuguese
Monetary Unit:	Escudo

BEEF ON A SPIT
Servings: 6

Ingredients:

900 g	*2 lb*	*beef kebabs*

Method:

1. The secret of this recipe is in marinating the meat well before cooking. Place beef kebabs in one of the following marinate for at least 24 hours (48 hours is better). Then string meat on skewers and grill over hot coals, turning occasionally, for 10-20 minutes, as desired.

Wine-Spice Marinade

250	*mL*	*1 c*	*dry red wine*
125	*mL*	*½ c*	*olive oil*
1		*1*	*bay leaf, crushed*
2		*2*	*garlic cloves, sliced*
			salt
			pepper
			allspice
			cumin
			paprika

Lemon-Garlic Marinade

1		*1*	*lemon, juice of*
125	*mL*	*½ c*	*olive oil*
2		*2*	*garlic cloves, sliced*
			salt
			pepper

MALAWI

Location: Africa
Captial City: Lilongwe
Language: English, Chichewa
Monetary Unit: Kwacha

CORNMEAL PORRIDGE
Servings: 4

Ingredients:

180	mL	¾ c	cornmeal
30	mL	2 T	butter
750	mL	3 c	milk
80	mL	⅓ c	cottage cheese
			salt

Method:

1. Melt the butter in a saucepan. Add cornmeal and roast without burning.

2. Pour milk over cornmeal mixture. Stir well to get a lump-free consistency. Add salt and cheese, lower heat to minimum, cover, and let simmer until porridge is done.

MALAYSIA

Location:	Asia
Captial City:	Kuala Lumpur
Language:	Malay, English
Monetary Unit:	Ringgit

SPINACH WITH PORK AND EGGS
Servings: 6

Ingredients:

1	kg	2	lb	fresh spinach
500	g	1	lb	lean pork, cubed
30	mL	2	T	soy sauce
30	mL	2	T	sherry
5	mL	1	t	brown sugar
2	mL	½	t	black pepper
45	mL	3	T	peanut oil
4		4		scallions, chopped
1		1		garlic clove, crushed
250	mL	1	c	water
3		3		eggs, beaten

Method:

1. Combine soy sauce, sherry, brown sugar and black pepper. Marinate meat at least 2 hours at room temperature.

2. Heat oil, saute scallions, garlic and meat until meat is brown. Add marinating and water. Bring to a boil. Cover, reduce heat and cook until meat is almost tender. Add spinach. Cover and continue cooking until spinach is cooked.

3. Beat eggs with salt. Pour mixture over spinach. Stir constantly until the egg is cooked.

4. Serve immediately.

79

MARTINIQUE

Location:	Caribbean Islands
Port City:	Port-de-France
Language:	French
Monetary Unit:	Franc

CRAB MEAT OMELETS
Servings: 2

Ingredients:

4		4		eggs
60	mL	1/4	c	milk
				pepper
				salt
60	mL	4	T	butter
180	g	6	oz	crab meat, flaked
30	mL	1/8	c	parsley, chopped
30	mL	1/8	c	celery, finely chopped
30	mL	1/8	c	onion, finely chopped
60	mL	1/4	c	mushroom, sliced
				salt
				paprika
				cayenne pepper
30	mL	1	T	cooking sherry

Method:

1. Saute the onion, celery and mushroom until tender. Add crab meat and parsley. Stir well. Season with salt, paprika and cayenne pepper. Stir in sherry, mix well and set aside.

2. Beat eggs in a bowl. Add milk, salt and pepper. Make two omelets.

3. Place half the filling in the centre of each omelet. Fold omlet in thirds to enclosed filling.

4. Serve immediately.

MAURITANIA

Location: Africa
Captial City: Nouakchott
Language: Arabic, French
Monetary Unit: Ouguyia

FISH DAUBE
Servings: 4

Ingredients:

500	g	1	lb	fish
500	g	1	lb	tomatoes, chopped
1		1		large onion, sliced
3		3		garlic cloves, crushed
1		1		chili pepper, chopped
½		½		bunch of parsley, chopped
½		½		bunch of thyme, chopped
30	mL	2	T	oil
				dash of crushed ginger
				salt
				white pepper
				oil for frying

Method:

1. Cut fish into 2.5 cm (1 inch) pieces. Season with salt and pepper and fry.

2. Fry onion in 30 mL (2 T) oil, add ginger, garlic and tomatoes and cook for 15 minutes on a low heat.

3. Add chilies, thyme, parsley and fried fish.

4. If necessary add 30 mL (2 T) water and cook for 5 minutes further with the lid on.

5. Serve with baked potato or rice.

MEXICO

Location: North America
Captial City: Mexico City
Language: Spanish
Monetary Unit: Peso

BLACK-BEAN SOUP
Servings: 6

Ingredients:

250	mL	1	c	dry black beans
2	l	2	qt	cold water
60	mL	4	T	oil
1		1		medium onion, chopped
1		1		garlic clove, chopped
2	mL	½	t	chili
125	mL	½	c	canned tomatoes, chopped
1	mL	¼	t	oregano
80	mL	⅓	c	dry sherry
				salt
				pepper

Method:

1. Wash beans, but do not soak them. Place in a large saucepan with water; cover and cook gently until almost tender.

2. In a skillet, heat oil, add onion, garlic and chili. When onion is tender but not browned, stir in tomato.

3. Combine this mixture with beans, oregano and salt and pepper to taste. Simmer covered until beans are very tender.

4. Push beans through a sieve or puree in a blender. Return to saucepan; simmer a few minutes longer; stir in sherry.

5. Serve with tortillas or crumbled fresh cheese.

MOROCCO

Location:	Africa
Captial City:	Rabat
Language:	Arabic, French, Spanish
Monetary Unit:	Dirham

ALMOND MILKSHAKE
Servings: 4

Ingredients:

250	mL	1	c	ground almond
125	mL	½	c	sugar
1	L	4	c	milk

Method:

1. Place ground almond, sugar and the milk into a blender. Cover and process until smooth.

2. Serve chilled.

NEPAL

Location: Asia
Captial City: Katmandu
Language: Nepali
Monetary Unit: Nepalese Rupee

FLOUR DESSERT
Servings: 4

Ingredients:

125	mL	½ c	unsalted butter
250	mL	1 c	all purpose flour
500	mL	2 c	milk
250	mL	1 c	sugar
60	mL	¼ c	chopped almonds

Method:

1. Make a syrup by boiling sugar in milk.

2. Melt butter in a pan. Add almonds and flour. Stir constantly over medium heat until flour becomes golden brown.

3. Pour boiling milk syrup into browned flour. Cook mixture for about 15 minutes on a very low heat. Remove from heat.

4. When mixture has cooled off, it can be shaped either by hand or by a spoon.

NETHERLANDS

Location: Europe
Captial City: Amsterdam
Language: Dutch
Monetary Unit: Guilder

DUTCH PEA SOUP
Servings: 8

Ingredients:

500	mL	2	c	split green peas
1.5	l	3	qt	cold water
1		1		pig's trotter
1		1		pig's ear
250	mL	1	c	bacon squares
4		4		Frankfurters
500	g	1	lb	potatoes, sliced
60	mL	4	T	salt
500	mL	2	c	celery, chopped
1		1		bunch celery green, cut up
2		2		leeks, cut up
2		2		onions
				salt

Method:

1. Wash the peas, soak for 12 hours (unless you use quick boiling peas) and boil gently in the water they were soaked in for at least 2 hours.

2. Cook the trotter, the ear and the bacon in this liquid for one hour. Add potatoes, salt, celery, celery leaves and leeks. Cook until everything is done or soup is smooth and thick. Lift out the trotter and discard skin and bones. Add meat bits to soup. Half an hour before serving add frankfurters.

3. The longer the soup simmers the better the taste. Three hours is the usual time in Holland. The soup is so thick when it cools that it can be cut the next day. That is the reason it is made in such big quantities.

4. Serve with pumpernickel bread.

NEW ZEALAND

Location: Oceania
Captial City: Wellington
Language: English, Maori
Monetary Unit: New Zealand Dollar

KIWI CHANTILLY
Servings: 4

Ingredients:

4		4		kiwi fruits
30	mL	2	T	kirsch
12		12		marshmallows
250	mL	1	c	cream
30	mL	2	T	icing sugar

Method:

1. Peel kiwis and slice or dice. Sprinkle with kirsch and let stand 1 hour.

2. Chop marshmallows and mix with fruit.

3. Whip together cream and icing sugar and carefully fold in fruit and marshmallows.

4. Serve in individual dishes accompanied with sweet biscuits or wafers.

NICARAGUA

Location: Central America
Captial City: Managua
Language: Spanish
Monetary Unit: Cordoba

NICARAGUAN RICE
Servings: 4

Ingredients:

250	mL	1 c	converted rice
250	mL	1 c	hot water
60	mL	1/4 c	butter
1		1	medium onion, chopped
1		1	small green pepper, chopped
2		2	medium tomatoes, chopped
			salt

Method:

1. Wash the rice with hot water and rinse it with cold water.

2. Saute the rice and onion in butter until onion is golden brown.

3. Add pepper, tomatoes, water and salt. Bring to a boil. Cover, reduce heat to very low. Cook for 10 minutes. Stir and cook another 10 minutes.

NIGER

Location:	Africa
Captial City:	Niamey
Language:	French
Monetary Unit:	Franc CFA

MEAT STEW
Servings: 4

Ingredients:

1	kg	2	lb	stewing beef
8		8		large tomatoes, sliced
4		4		medium onions, sliced
60	mL	4	T	peanut or corn oil
750	mL	3	c	water
				salt
				cummin powder
				black pepper

Method:

1. Fry onions until soft. Remove from saucepan. Place meat in saucepan and brown. Add water, cover and cook over low heat until water is reduced by ⅔ and meat is tender.

2. Add onions, tomatoes, salt, pepper and cummin. Simmer for half an hour.

3. Serve hot with boiled rice.

NIGERIA

Location: Africa
Captial City: Lagos
Language: English
Monetary Unit: Naira

GROUNDNUT STEW
Servings: 4

Ingredients:

950	g	2	lb	beef, cut into cubes
3		3		onions, chopped
2		2		garlic cloves, crushed
450	g	½ lb		groundnuts, shelled or
250	g	9 oz		peanut butter
1		1		red bell pepper, chopped
45	mL	3	T	oil
500	mL	2	c	water
				salt
				black pepper

Method:

1. Fry onions and garlic until tender, not brown. Add meat and continue frying until brown. Add water, salt and pepper. Cover and cook over low heat until meat is tender.

2. Meanwhile roast groundnuts and remove skins. Roll them on a board to a very smooth paste. Mix to a paste with a little water. Add this or peanut butter and red pepper to stew. Continue cooking for half an hour.

3. Serve hot with rice, potatoes or boiled yam.

NORWAY

Location: Europe
Captial City: Oslo
Language: Norwegian, Lappish
Monetary Unit: Krone

FISH PUDDING
Servings: 4

Ingredients:

750	g	1 ½ lb	*fresh fillets of cod, cubed*
180	mL	¾ c	*light cream*
180	mL	¾ c	*heavy cream*
30	mL	2 T	*cornstarch*
			ground nutmeg
			black pepper
			salt
			fine bread crumbs
			butter
			parsley
			paprika

Method:

1. Butter fish mold and sprinkle with bread crumbs. Set aside.

2. In a food processor or a blender, blend fish, seasoning and cornstarch, while slowly adding light and heavy cream until smooth and fluffy.

3. Poor fish mixture into the mold. Cover tightly with buttered aluminum foil. Place the mold in a large baking pan and place in middle of oven. Add boiling water to outside pan to cover half the mold.

4. Bake 180°C (350°F) for 45 minutes or until a knife inserted into the centre of pudding comes out clean. Prevent water boiling by reducing heat about 15°C (25°F).

5. Take mold out of pan and let stand for 5 minutes. Pour off any liquid in mold, then unmold to a warm serving plate. Garnish with parsley and paprika.

6. Serve with buttered boiled potatoes.

OMAN

Location: Asia
Captial City: Muskat
Language: Arabic
Monetary Unit: Omani Rial

OMANI RICE
Servings: 4

Ingredients:

500	mL	2	c	basmati rice
950	mL	4	c	water
3		3		onions, sliced
60	mL	4	T	butter
				salt
				saffron

Method:

1. Soak rice in slightly salted hot water then drain and rinse with cold water.

2. Soak a pinch of saffron in 125 mL (½ c) warm water.

3. Boil water and salt. Add rice, bring back to a boil, and boil for two minutes. Drain.

4. Place onions on bottom of pot. Add melted butter and drained rice. Pour saffron over rice. Place over medium high heat until rice is steaming. Then simmer for at least 25 minutes.

PAKISTAN

Location: Asia
Captial City: Islamabad
Language: English, Urdu
Monetary Unit: Pakistani Rupee

SPICY LAMB
Servings: 6

Ingredients:

1	kg	2	lb	boneless lamb shoulder
3		3		large onions, chopped
3		3		garlic cloves, chopped
5	mL	1	t	ground ginger
2		½	t	ground turmeric
3		3		large tomatoes, skinned, choppe
7	mL	½	T	coriander seeds
7	mL	½	T	cummin seeds
30	mL	2	T	desiccated coconut
80	mL	⅓	c	oil
2	mL	½	t	cardamom seeds
4		4		whole cloves
1	mL	¼	t	black pepper
2		2		bay leaves
1		1		cinnamon stick
125	mL	½	c	yogurt
				water

Method:
1. In a pan, dry roast coriander, cumin and coconut over medium heat for 2 minutes. Toss frequently. Set aside.

2. Blend onion, garlic, turmeric, ginger and tomatoes until they make a smooth paste. Set aside.

3. Heat 60 mL (4 T) of oil in a pan. Add cardamom, cloves, cinnamon, bay leaves and pepper. Fry for about 1 minute, then add a few pieces of lamb at a time and brown. When all meat is done, remove from pan, cover and set aside.

4. Add remaining oil to same pan, then add the onion tomato paste. Cook for 3 minutes. Add the roasted spices and cook for 2 minutes. Stir in yogurt a little at a time. Add lamb and salt. Cover with water, bring to a boil. Cover and simmer over low heat about 1 hour or until meat is tender. Remove cinnamon stick, cloves and bay leaves.

5. Transfer to a warm serving dish and serve with rice.

PANAMA

Location: Central America
Captial City: Panama City
Language: Spanish
Monetary Unit: Balboa

FISH IN VEGETABLE SAUCE
Servings: 4

Ingredients:

4		*4*		*fillets of sea trout*
125	*mL*	*½ c*		*flour*
				salt
				black pepper
45	*mL*	*3*	*T*	*butter*
1		*1*		*Spanish onion, chopped*
2		*2*		*garlic cloves, minced*
1		*1*		*celery stalks, sliced*
1		*1*		*green pepper, chopped*
2		*2*		*large tomatoes, chopped*
30	*mL*	*2*	*T*	*pimento, chopped*
30	*mL*	*2*	*T*	*parsley, chopped*
30	*mL*	*2*	*T*	*capers*
125	*mL*	*½ c*		*water*
				salt
				pepper

Method:

1. Cut fillets in half and dip in a mixture of flour, salt and black pepper.

2. In a large skillet melt butter, saute the onion, garlic and celery until golden. Add green pepper, tomatoes, water, salt and pepper. Cook over low heat 15 minutes, then add fillets. Cover and cook until fish is almost tender.

3. Sprinkle with parsley, pimento and capers and cook 2 minutes.

PARAGUAY

Location: South America
Captial City: Asuncion
Language: Spanish, Guarani
Monetary Unit: Guarani

NOODLES WITH MUSHROOMS
Servings: 4

Ingredients:

6	6	slices of bacon
250 g	½ lb	fresh mushrooms, sliced
125 g	¼ lb	pepperoni, thinly sliced
250 g	½ lb	tomatoes, peeled, chopped
½	½	Spanish onion, finely chopped
125 mL	½ c	water
		salt
950 mL	4 c	cooked wide noodles

Method:

1. In a Dutch oven, fry bacon until crisp. Remove and crumble.

2. Saute onion in drippings until tender. Add mushrooms, pepperoni, tomatoes, salt and water. Cook over low heat for 15 minutes. Stir occasionally. Add noodles, heat gently.

3. Remove to a heated platter and garnish with bacon crisp.

PERU

Location: South America
Capital City: Lima
Language: Spanish, Quechua
Monetary Unit: Inti

SCALLOP SHRIMP CASSEROLE
Servings: 4

Ingredients:

250	g	½ lb	scallops
250	g	½ lb	shrimp, deveined
125	mL	½ c	green onion, sliced
60	mL	4 T	butter
30	mL	2 T	flour
60	mL	¼ c	water
250	mL	1 c	milk
125	mL	½ c	heavy cream
			salt
			cayenne pepper
			ground nutmeg

Method:

1. Fry onions with pepper and nutmeg in butter until golden; then add flour, stirring constantly, fry 2 more minutes. Remove from heat, add water stir until lump free.

2. Add milk, scallops and shrimp. Return to low heat, cook until shrimp are tender. Add salt and cream. Stir well.

3. Serve with mashed potato or rice.

PHILIPPINES

Location: Asia
Capital City: Manila
Language: English, Philipino
Monetary Unit: Peso

BRAISED CHICKEN AND PORK
Servings: 4

Ingredients:

500	g	1	lb	boneless lean pork, cubed
4		4		chicken legs
125	mL	½	c	rice vinegar
2		2		garlic cloves, minced
30	mL	2	T	soy sauce
1		1		bay leaf
				salt
				black pepper
60	mL	¼	c	oil
60	mL	¼	c	water

Method:

1. Place chicken and pork in a glass bowl. Add vinegar, bay leaf, garlic, soy sauce, salt and pepper. Cover and refrigerate for 2 days, turning meat occasionally.

2. Place meat, marinating liquid and water to a pan. Bring to a boil. Reduce heat and simmer covered until meat is tender. Remove meat to paper towel and pat dry.

3. Discard bay leaf. Thicken the sauce and keep it warm.

4. Saute meat in oil until well browned. Place on a serving dish, pouring sauce over meat.

5. Serve warm with rice.

POLAND

Location:	Europe
Capital City:	Warsaw
Language:	Polish
Monetary Unit:	Zloty

ROLLED VEAL CUTLETS
Servings: 6

Ingredients:

12		12		*thin medium size veal cutlets*
1		1		*large onion, minced*
500	mL	2	c	*soft bread crumbs*
2		2		*eggs*
45	mL	3	T	*butter*
500	mL	2	c	*beef stock*
				oil for frying
				salt
				pepper
				flour
				parsley

Method:

1. Sprinkle cutlets with salt and pepper.

2. Beat egg slightly, combine with bread crumbs, onion and melted butter. Season with salt and pepper.

3. Spread mixture on cutlets. Roll up and tie with string. Dredge with flour and brown in oil. Pour beef stock over meat. Bring to a boil, cover and simmer over moderate heat until meat is tender.

4. Remove strings and place roll-ups on a heated platter. Pour gravy over meat, decorate with chopped parsley. Serve with mashed potatoes.

PORTUGAL

Location: Europe
Capital City: Lisbon
Language: Portuguese
Monetary Unit: Escudo

COD WITH RICE
Servings: 8

Ingredients:

1	kg	2	lb	salted cod
3		3		medium onion, chopped
2		2		garlic cloves, crushed
500	g	1	lb	tomatoes, skinned, chopped
125	mL	½	c	olive oil
30	mL	2	T	chopped parsley
60	mL	¼	c	dry white wine
1		1		pimento, diced
				black pepper
				water
250	mL	1	c	rice

Method:

1. Soak salted cod overnight. Drain. Add fresh water, bring to a boil and cook 10 minutes. Remove and cut into large cubes.

2. Cook rice in boiling water. Drain and keep warm.

3. In a skillet, fry onion in oil until transparent. Add fish, garlic, tomatoes, pimento, parsley, pepper and wine. Cover and simmer over very low heat for 45 minutes or until fish is tender.

4. Remove fish onto a serving dish. Keep warm. Add boiled rice to sauce. Stir well. Pour the mixture around the fish. Serve immediately.

PUERTO RICO

Location:	Caribbean
Port City:	San Huan
Language:	English, Spanish
Monetary Unit:	USA Dollar

BAKED EGG CUSTARD
Servings: 8

Ingredients:

125	mL	½ c		sugar
500	mL	2 c		evaporated milk
125	mL	½ c		milk
7		7		eggs, slightly beaten
250	mL	1	c	sugar
10	mL	2	t	vanilla
				dash of salt

Method:

1. Melt 125 mL (½ c) sugar in a small pan. Stir slowly until it turns golden. Pour into a 1 L (4 c) mold. Set aside.

2. Scald milk with 250 mL (1 c) sugar. Add vanilla and salt. Combine eggs and milk. Pour into caramelized mold.

3. Place mold in a large pan. Add boiling water to ½ height of the mold. Bake in a 163°C (325°F) oven for one hour. Cool, cover and refrigerate overnight.

4. Run a knife around the sides, unmold over a serving dish.

QATAR

Location: Asia
Capital City: Doha
Language: Arabic
Monetary Unit: Qatari Riyal

FISH IN SESAME SAUCE
Servings: 4

Ingredients:

1	*kg*	*2*	*lb*	*fish fillets*
125	*mL*	*½*	*c*	*ground sesame (tahini)*
60	*mL*	*4*	*T*	*olive oil*
30	*mL*	*2*	*T*	*fresh lemon juice*
125	*mL*	*½*	*c*	*water*
2		*2*		*large onions, chopped*
				salt
				black pepper

Method:

1. Mix lemon juice, water and tahini to make a smooth sauce.

2. Saute onions in 45 mL (3 T) oil.

3. Rub fish fillets with salt, black pepper and a tablespoon of olive oil. Place in an oiled baking dish and bake uncovered for 15 minutes at 180°C (350°F) or until fish is flaky.

4. Pour sesame sauce and sauteed onion over baked fish. Continue baking for another 15 minutes.

5. Serve warm with green salad.

ROMANIA

Location:	Europe
Capital City:	Bucharest
Language:	Romanian, Magyar, Turkish
Monetary Unit:	Leu

ROMANIAN HAMBURGER
Servings: 4

Ingredients:

500	g	1	lb	regular ground beef
5		5		garlic cloves, minced
5	mL	1	t	cummin
5	mL	1	t	allspice
5	mL	1	t	black pepper
10	mL	2	t	ground rosemary
5	mL	1	t	baking powder
				salt
60	mL	1/4	c	water
30	mL	2	T	olive oil

Method:

1. Put all ingredients except oil in a mixing bowl. Mix with hands about 20 minutes. Cover and refrigerate overnight.

2. Roll the mixture by hand into mini-balls, then press to form hamburger patties. Brush with oil.

3. Place hamburgers on an oiled barbecue grate 15 cm (6 inch) above hot coals. Grill one side until crisp and brown, then turn over.

4. Serve with green salad.

SAUDI ARABIA

Location: Asia
Capital City: Riyadh
Language: Arabic
Monetary Unit: Riyal

LENTIL SOUP
Servings: 6

Ingredients:

125	mL	½	c	brown lentils, washed
1.5	L	6	c	beef stock
15	mL	1	T	salt
30	mL	2	T	fresh lemon juice
1	mL	¼	t	cumin
125	mL	½	c	rice
500	mL	2	c	Swiss chard, shredded
2		2		large onions, chopped
45	mL	3	T	butter
				paprika

Method:

1. Place lentils, beef stock, salt, lemon juice, cumin and pepper in a pot. Bring to a boil. Reduce heat, cover and cook for 30 minutes. Add rice, bring back to a boil. Reduce heat, cover and simmer for 10 minutes.

2. Add Swiss chard and cook 10 more minutes. Set aside. Keep warm.

3. Saute onions in butter until golden. Add to soup and sprinkle with paprika.

SINGAPORE

Location:	Asia
Capital City:	Singapore
Language:	Malay, Chinese, English
Monetary Unit:	Singapore Dollar

SPRING ROLLS
Servings: 20

Ingredients:

20		20		spring roll wrappers
				oil for frying
1		1		medium onion, minced
1		1		garlic clove, minced
5	mL	1	t	fresh ginger, grated
5		5		dried mushrooms
5		5		water chestnuts, chopped
250	mL	1	c	bamboo shoots, shredded
250	mL	1	c	Chinese cabbage, shredded
250	g	½ lb		bean sprouts
250	g	½ lb		minced pork
250	g	½ lb		raw shrimp, peeled, deveined, chopped
30	mL	2	T	soy sauce
30	mL	2	T	vegetable oil
15	mL	1	T	sesame oil
15	mL	1	T	corn starch
30	mL	2	T	water
				salt and black pepper

Method:

1. Cover mushrooms with fresh water and soak for 1 hour. Drain, remove stalks and chop mushrooms.

2. Meanwhile, marinate pork with 15 mL (1 T) soy sauce and pepper for 1 hour.

3. Heat wok, add vegetable and sesame oil. Saute garlic and onions then ginger. Add pork and shrimp and stir fry. Put cabbage, chestnuts, bamboo shoots, mushrooms, balance of soy sauce and salt. Mix well and continue stir frying.

4. Dissolve cornstarch in water and add to mixture. Stir well and cover for 2 minutes. Add bean sprouts, toss and remove from heat, and cool.

5. Place one heaping tablespoon of mixture on each wrap, roll up, seal the edges with water and deep fry until golden.

SOUTH AFRICA

Location: Africa
Capital City: Cape Town
Language: Afrikaans, English
Monetary Unit: Rand

LENTIL SHEPHERD'S PIE
Servings: 4

Ingredients:

250	mL	1	c	lentils
1		1		medium onion, chopped
1	mL	¼	t	sage
5	mL	1	t	parsley
5	mL	1	t	salt
				cayenne pepper
500	mL	2	c	water
1		1		large potato, boiled
30	mL	2	T	hot milk
15	mL	1	T	melted butter
				salt

Method:

1. Cook lentils in water and salt mixture until all water is absorbed.

2. In a mixing bowl, mash cooked lentils. Add onions and seasoning; place in a lightly oiled casserole dish.

3. In a separate bowl, mash potato and add milk, butter and salt. Beat until fluffy.

4. Spread on top of lentils and bake for 20 minutes in an oven heated at 200°C (400°F).

5. A good vegetarian dish. May be served with rice and salad.

SPAIN

Location:	Europe
Capital City:	Madrid
Language:	Spanish, Basque, Catalan
Monetary Unit:	Peseta

STUFFED SOLE
Servings: 4

Ingredients:

8		8	sole fillets
250	g	½ lb	cooked shrimp, chopped finely
125	mL	½ c	white sauce, thick
			salt
			paprika
			white pepper
2		2	eggs
			bread crumbs
			oil for frying

Method:

1. Mix the shrimp with white sauce; season and divide into 8.

2. Fill fillets with sauce and shrimp mixture. Roll up and tie with string.

3. Beat eggs. Dip fillet rolls first in egg, then in bread crumbs. Fry in deep oil until golden, then cut string.

4. Serve immediately with tartar sauce.

SRI LANKA

Location:	Asia
Capital City:	Colombo
Language:	Sinhala, English, Tamil
Monetary Unit:	Sri Lanka Rupee

VEAL CURRY
Servings: 6

Ingredients:

1	kg	2	lb	boneless veal chunks
3		3		onions, sliced
3		3		garlic cloves, minced
2	mL	½ t		chili powder
10	mL	2 t		paprika
5	mL	1 t		ground coriander
2	mL	½ t		ground cumin
2	mL	½ t		ground cinnamon
2	mL	½ t		ground ginger
				pinch of turmeric
				salt
60	mL	¼ c		vinegar
250	mL	1 c		thick coconut milk (see page 71)
60	mL	¼ c		oil

Method:

1. Place meat in a Dutch oven. Add the onion, garlic, spices and seasoning. Cover with water, then add vinegar. Bring to a boil. Cover, reduce heat and simmer 1 hour or until meat is tender. Add coconut milk and simmer another 15 minutes uncovered.

2. Remove meat and keep sauce hot.

3. Fry meat in oil until brown. Transfer to a serving plate. Pour sauce over meat.

4. Serve with rice.

SUDAN

Location:	Africa
Capital City:	Khartoum
Language:	Arabic, English
Monetary Unit:	Sudanese Pound

OKRA STEW WITH LAMB
Servings: 4

Ingredients:

250	g	½	lb	fresh or frozen okra
250	g	½	lb	lean lamb meat, cut in small pieces
1		1		medium onion, chopped finely
45	mL	3	T	butter
45	mL	3	T	tomato paste
500	mL	2	c	water
15	mL	1	T	lemon juice
				salt
				black pepper

Method:

1. Saute onions in butter until golden; then add meat, salt, pepper and tomato paste and cook slowly until all sides are brown. Add water, bring to a boil, then simmer covered for 45 minutes.

2. Add okra and lemon juice and cook until okra and meat are tender.

3. Serve hot with rice pilaff.

SURINAME

Location:	South America
Capital City:	Paramaribo
Language:	Dutch, Surinamese
Monetary Unit:	Surinamese Guilder

PINEAPPLE CAKE
Servings: 6

Ingredients:

500	mL	2	c	pineapple filling

Dough:

60	mL	¼ c	milk
110	g	¼ lb	butter
225	g	½ lb	flour
15	mL	1 T	sugar
1	mL	¼ t	vanilla

Batter:

8		8		eggs
125	mL	½ c		sugar
125	mL	½ c		flour
1	mL	¼ t		vanilla
135	mL	9 t		butter, melted, cooled

Method:

1. Combine flour, sugar, butter, milk and vanilla to make dough. Knead until a firm ball is formed. Roll it out to place on buttered bottom of a baking dish.

2. Spread the pineapple filling over dough.

3. Make batter by beating eggs with sugar until foamy; then add vanilla. Add flour one spoon at a time, blending well after each addition. Add melted butter and mix lightly.

4. Pour batter over pineapple filling and bake in a previously heated moderate oven (180°C or 350°F) for 40 minutes.

   Do not open oven during the first 20 minutes.

SWEDEN

Location:	Europe
Port City:	Stockholm
Language:	Swedish, Finnish
Monetary Unit:	Krona

VEAL IN DILL SAUCE
Servings: 4

Ingredients:

1	kg	2	lb	breast, leg or shoulder of veal, cut into small cubes
				salt
6		6		peppercorns
1		1		medium onion, chopped
1		1		leek, chopped
2		2		carrots, chopped
125	mL	½	c	celery, chopped
15	mL	1	T	dried dill

Dill Sauce:

30	mL	2	T	butter
30	mL	2	T	flour
500	mL	2	c	stock
125	mL	½	c	heavy cream
30	mL	2	T	dried dill
20	mL	4	t	white vinegar
10	mL	2	t	sugar
2		2		egg yolks

Method:

1. Place meat in a casserole dish. Add salt, peppercorns and enough water to cover meat. Bring to a boil and scum surface. Add vegetables and dill. Cover and simmer slowly for 1.5 hours or until meat is very tender. Strain and boil down stock to 500 mL (2 c).

2. For sauce: melt butter, add flour and stir until well blended. Blend in stock gradually while stirring, and let sauce boil for 3 minutes. Add vinegar and sugar.
   In a stainless steel pan, cook egg yolks and cream over low heat until thickened. Do not boil. Remove from heat, blend into sauce and add dill.

3. Pour sauce over meat or serve separately along with buttered boiled potatoes or rice and peas.

SWITZERLAND

Location: Europe
Capital City: Bern
Language: German, French, Italian
Monetary Unit: Swiss Franc

CHEESE AND ONION PIE
Servings: 4

Ingredients:

250	g	½ lb		Swiss cheese, grated
2		2		large onion, sliced
15	mL	1	T	flour
3		3		eggs, beaten
250	mL	1	c	milk or cream
				salt
				pepper
1		1		unbaked 23 cm (9 inch) pie crust

Method:

1. Saute onions in butter and set aside.

2. Dredge cheese with flour. Beat eggs well and mix with milk. Season lightly. Pour mixture with cheese.

3. Distribute sauteed onion evenly on the pie shell then add cheese mixture.

4. Bake 15 minutes in 200°C (400°F) oven, then reduce heat to 150°C (300°F). Bake until knife inserted in centre comes out clean, about 25 minutes.

5. Serve hot with vegetable soup to start, a mixed salad with pie, and fresh fruit and coffee.

SYRIA

Location: Asia
Capital City: Damascus
Language: Arabic
Monetary Unit: Syrian Pound

BULGUR PILAFF
Servings: 4

Ingredients:

250	mL	1	c	bulgur wheat
1		1		Spanish onion, sliced
45	mL	3	T	butter
5		5		canned tomatoes, chopped
				salt
				black pepper
375	mL	1 ½	c	meat broth

Method:

1. Saute onion and bulgur in butter over medium heat about 15 minutes.

2. Add tomatoes, salt and pepper and meat broth. Mix well, cover and cook over medium heat until liquid has evaporated.

3. Serve hot with kebabs or yogurt.

TANZANIA

Location:	Africa
Capital City:	Dar-es-Salaam
Language:	Swahili, Arabic, English
Monetary Unit:	Tanzanian Shilling

TANZANIAN PILAFF
Servings: 4

Ingredients:

250	mL	1	c	Basmati rice
1		1		onion, finely chopped
4		4		garlic cloves, crushed
1		1		cinnamon stick
5	mL	1	t	whole black pepper
5	mL	1	t	ground cumin
5	mL	1	t	ground ginger
6		6		whole cloves
250	gr	½	lb	cooked stewing beef chopped in small pieces
1		1		potato, chopped in small cubes (optional)
125	mL	½	c	raisins
45	mL	3	T	vegetable oil
				salt
				roasted cashew nuts or almonds

Method:

1. Soak rice in water for 15 minutes. Preheat oven to 190°C (375°F).

2. Saute onion in vegetable oil until translucent. Add garlic and allspice. Stir and saute until onion and garlic are golden. Add potato and beef. Cook for one minute. Stir well.

3. Rinse rice and add to frying mixture. Stir well. Add boiling water and salt to taste. Cook uncovered over slow heat for 10 to 15 minutes. (If the rice becomes too dry, add more boiling water and continue to cook over very low heat until all water evaporates.) Add raisins, mix well.

4. Place in an ovenproof dish, cover and bake for 20 minutes.

5. Garnish with cashew nuts or almonds and serve hot.

THAILAND

Location:	Asia
Capital City:	Bangkok
Language:	Thai, Chinese, English
Monetary Unit:	Baht

SHRIMP SOUP WITH LIME
Servings: 2

Ingredients:

750	mL	3	c	water or fish broth
2		2		takrai (lemon grass)
				cut into 2.5 cm (1 inch) pieces
½		½		galanga root, crushed
2		2		kaffir (lime leaves), whole
3		3		whole shallots, peeled
3		3		whole garlic cloves, peeled
1		1		dried red chili, crushed
250	mL	1	c	fresh shrimp, shelled, deveined
30	mL	2	T	nam pla (fish's gravy)
15	mL	1	T	lime juice
5	mL	1	t	sugar
5	mL	1	t	fresh coriander, chopped
½		½		fresh red chili, cut into fine strips

Method:

1. Bring water or fish broth to a boil.

2. Using a square of cheesecloth, tie up lemon grass, galanga, lime leaves, shallots, garlic and chili and put into liquid. Cover and simmer 20 minutes.

3. Add shrimp and continue simmering until they are pink and curled, about 5 minutes.

4. Remove cheesecloth bag and add nam pla, lime juice and sugar.

5. Decorate with coriander and red chili strips. Serve hot.

TOGO

Location: Africa
Capital City: Lome
Language: French
Monetary Unit: Franc CFA

LAMB AND SEAFOOD STEW
Servings: 4

Ingredients:

250	gr	½ lb		shrimp, sliced
250	gr	½ lb		crab meat, sliced
250	gr	½ lb		smoked fish
250	gr	½ lb		lamb, cubed
60	mL	¼ c		crushed ground nuts
2		2		medium onions, finely chopped
2		2		large tomatoes, chopped
30	mL	2	T	oil
2		2		cloves
1	mL	¼ t		red pepper
2	mL	½ t		dry mustard
				dash of aniseed
				salt
				water

Method:

1. Put lamb in a pan, cover with water. Add salt, a little bit of onion and tomatoes. Bring to a boil. Cover and simmer for 20 minutes. Set aside.

2. In a separate pot, poach the smoked fish for 15 minutes, then set aside.

3. Boil shrimp and crab meat for 5 minutes in water to which red pepper, salt and mustard have been added. Remove and reserve liquid.

4. Saute onions, aniseed and cloves in oil until onions are golden. Add lamb mixture, fish, shrimp and crab meat. Stir gently. Pour in shrimp and crab meat stock. Add crushed ground nuts and simmer for ½ hour partly covered.

5. Serve warm with corn bread.

TRINIDAD AND TOBAGO

Location:	Carribeans
Capital City:	Port-of-Spain
Language:	English, Hindi, French
Monetary Unit:	Trinidad and Tobago Dollar

CALYPSO PUNCH
Servings: 10

Ingredients:

950	mL	4	c	grapefruit juice
75	mL	5	T	lime juice
5	mL	1	t	bitters
500	mL	2	c	rum (optional)
6		6		slices orange
250	mL	1	c	pineapple juice
125	mL	½	c	lemon juice
500	mL	2	c	plain syrup
3		3		green lime rinds
500	mL	2	c	water

Method:

1. Combine lemon and lime juice, blend well. Stir in rum, add bitters.

2. Combine grapefruit juice, pineapple juice, plain syrup and water.

3. Combine both mixtures and chill.

4. Just before serving, pour over ice cubes in punch bowl. Decorate with green rinds of lime and orange slices.

TUNISIA

Location:	Africa
Capital City:	Tunis
Language:	Arabic, French
Monetary Unit:	Tunisian Dinar

SEA BASS CASSEROLE
Servings: 4

Ingredients:

4		4	sea bass fillets
			black pepper
			salt
60	mL	1/4 c	olive oil
80	mL	1/3 c	fresh lemon juice
60	mL	4 T	oil
1		1	Spanish onion, sliced
12		12	canned tomatoes, chopped
12		12	small new potatoes, peeled
12		12	pearls onions, peeled
500	mL	2 c	chickpeas, cooked
500	mL	2 c	clam juice or fish stock
1	mL	1/4 t	cayenne pepper
1	mL	1/4 t	saffron
250	mL	1 c	sultanas

Method:

1. Marinate fillets in olive oil, lemon juice, salt and pepper mixture for several hours. Transfer fillets to a baking dish, sprinkle with marinate.

2. Saute onions in oil until golden brown, then add tomatoes, potatoes, pearl onions, chickpeas, fish stock, cayenne pepper and saffron. Simmer until potatoes are tender.

3. Pour mixture over fish. Sprinkle with sultanas and bake in 180 °C (350°F) oven about 25 minutes.

TURKEY

Location:	Asia and Europe
Capital City:	Ankara
Language:	Turkish
Monetary Unit:	Turkish Lira

STUFFED MUSSELS
Servings: 6

Ingredients:

24		24		large fresh mussels
125	mL	½ c		uncooked rice
3		3		large onions, chopped
125	mL	½ c		olive oil
125	mL	½ c		water
1		1		tomato, skinned, chopped
30	mL	2	T	pine nuts
30	mL	2	T	currants
7	mL	½	T	sugar
				salt
				black pepper
				allspice
500	mL	2	c	water

Method:

1. Soak mussels in salted water approximately 2 hours. Scrape and thoroughly wash mussel shells. Open without separating the two halves by inserting a butter knife and moving it towards pointed side of mussels. Remove hair of the each mussels, wash several times and soak in cold water.

2. In a saucepan, heat oil and saute onions until golden. Add washed rice and pine nuts and continue frying gently for 10 minutes. Add 125 mL (½ c) water, tomato, currant, sugar, salt, black pepper and allspice. Mix well, cover and cook over low heat for 15 to 20 minutes. Leave to cool in pan.

3. Stuff mussels, close down firmly and tie with string. Place stuffed mussels tightly in a heavy pan. Pour in 500 mL (2 c) of water. Put an inverted plate over mussels in order to keep them in place. Cover pan and cook over medium to high heat for 30 minutes. Remove from heat and leave to cool in pan.

4. Discard strings. Brush each mussel with a small amount of oil. Arrange on a serving dish, garnish with lemon wedges. Refrigerate and serve cold.

UGANDA

Location: Africa
Capital City: Kampala
Language: English, Swahili
Monetary Unit: Uganda Shilling

CREAM OF PEANUT SOUP
Servings: 8

Ingredients:

30	mL	2	T	cornstarch
750	mL	3	c	milk
750	mL	3	c	chicken stock, hot
500	mL	2	c	peanuts
30	mL	2	T	onion, grated
				salt
				cayenne pepper

Method:

1. Place cornstarch in a deep saucepan. Slowly add milk, stirring until smooth. Add stock, peanuts, onion, salt and cayenne pepper, stirring constantly.

2. Bring to a boil and cook over medium heat for 5 minutes. Place in a blender and blend for 2 minutes.

3. Serve hot.

UNION OF SOVIET SOCIALIST REPUBLICS

Location: Europe, Asia
Capital City: Moscow
Language: Slavic, Altaic
Monetary Unit: Ruble

BEEF STROGANOFF
Servings: 4

Ingredients:

500	g	1	lb	*fillet of beef, cut into strips*
45	mL	3	T	*butter*
30	mL	2	T	*flour*
250	mL	1	c	*broth*
125	mL	½	c	*water*
5	mL	1	t	*dry mustard*
15	mL	1	T	*tomato paste*
500	mL	2	c	*fresh mushroom, sliced*
				salt
				pepper
60	mL	¼	c	*sour cream*

Method:

1. In a saucepan, melt 15 mL (1 T) of butter, add flour and brown slightly. Stir in broth, water, mustard and tomato paste. Cook until thickened. Cover and set aside.

2. In a skillet, melt remaining butter. Saute onion and mushroom until just tender; then add meat and brown. Add salt, pepper and sauce. Cover and simmer until meat is tender.

3. In a bowl, beat sour cream with part of sauce from skillet, then pour mixture into skillet. Heat gently.

4. Serve with rice or boiled potatoes.

UNITED ARAB EMIRATES

Location: Asia
Capital City: Abu Dhabi
Language: Arabic, Farsi
Monetary Unit: Dirham

CHICKPEA SOUP
Servings: 6

Ingredients:

100	*g*	*¼ lb*	*chickpeas*
225	*g*	*½ lb*	*ground beef*
1		*1*	*small onion, minced*
1		*1*	*large tomato, skinned, chopped*
15	*mL*	*1 T*	*tomato paste*
2	*l*	*8 c*	*beef stock*
30	*mL*	*⅛ c*	*vine vinegar*
10	*mL*	*2 t*	*thyme*
			salt
			black pepper

Method:

1. Soak chickpeas overnight in salted water. Drain, rinse and boil in salted fresh water until tender. Drain and set aside.

2. Mix well together ground beef, onion, salt and pepper. Form into small balls. Cover and set aside.

3. In a heavy saucepan, boil beef stock, chickpeas, tomato, tomato paste and salt. Add meatballs, bring to a boil. Reduce heat, cover and cook until meatballs are tender.

4. Remove from heat, add vinegar and sprinkle with thyme. Stir well and serve hot.

UNITED KINGDOM

Location: Europe
Capital City: London
Language: English, Welsh, Gaelic
Monetary Unit: English Pound

TRIFLE
Servings: 6

Ingredients:

1	1	23 cm (9 inch) sponge cake
6	6	almond macaroons
180 mL	¾ c	raspberry jam
250 mL	1 c	sherry
250 mL	1 c	fresh or frozen fruit
500 mL	2 c	milk
125 mL	½ c	whipping cream
60 mL	4 T	cornstarch
5 mL	1 t	vanilla
80 mL	⅓ c	sugar
4	4	egg yolks
		pinch of salt
250 mL	1 c	whipping cream
30 mL	⅓ c	sugar
125 mL	½ c	slivered almonds
60 mL	¼ c	glaceed cherries

Method:

1. Break cake into small chunks, then crumble macaroons. Place both cake and maracroons in a dish, pour sherry evenly over mixture and soak for 20 minutes. Cover with jam, then spread fruit over mixture. Set aside.

2. In top of double boiler, gently heat milk, cream, cornstarch, sugar and salt mixture. Beat egg yolks. Add 125 mL (½ c) of hot milk sauce to egg yolks and mix well. Add mixture to remaining milk sauce. Cook and stir until thickened. Remove from heat, stir in vanilla. Cool.

3. Pour custard sauce over cake and fruit.

4. Whip cream with sugar and garnish top, then decorate with cherries and almonds.

UNITED STATES OF AMERICA

Location: North America
Capital City: Washington, D. C.
Language: English, Spanish
Monetary Unit: US Dollar

SPOON BREAD
Servings: 4

Ingredients:

500	mL	2	c	milk
125	mL	½	c	cornmeal
30	mL	2	T	butter
5	mL	1	t	salt
3		3		eggs, separated

Method:

1. In a double boiler scald milk. Gradually stir in cornmeal mixed with salt. Cook, stirring, until thick. Add butter and cool.

2. Beat egg yolks and white separately. Stir in egg yolks, then fold in egg whites. Pour into well greased baking dish.

3. Place baking dish in a large pan filled with warm water. Bake uncovered at 180°C (350°F) in a preheated oven for 45 minutes.

4. Serve at once from baking dish, spooning to dinner plates. May be served instead of rice or potatoes.

URUGUAY

Location: South America
Capital City: Montevideo
Language: Spanish
Monetary Unit: New Peso

STRING BEANS SALAD
Servings: 4

Ingredients:

450	g	1	lb	string beans
10	mL	2	t	salt
30	mL	2	T	butter
15	mL	1	T	lemon juice
30	mL	2	T	chopped parsley
1		1		garlic clove, minced
				salt
				black pepper

Method:

1. Wash beans. Shred and break in two. Boil quickly in salted water until beans are tender. When tender, wash beans in cold water two or three times.

2. Melt butter in a frying pan. Add garlic, beans, pepper and parsley. Stir fry for about 5 minutes.

3. Sprinkle with lemon juice when serving.

VENEZUELA

Location: South America
Capital City: Caracas
Language: Spanish
Monetary Unit: Bolivar

CORNMEAL CASSEROLE
Servings: 8

Ingredients:

250	g	½	lb		cooked round steak, diced
250	g	½	lb		cooked pork loin, diced
500	mL	2	c		cooked chicken, diced
30	mL	2	T		olive oil
125	mL	½	c		chopped onion
1		1			large green pepper, chopped
2		2			large tomatoes, chopped
2		2			garlic cloves, minced
60	mL	¼	c		chopped parsley
15	mL	1	T		bottled caper, chopped
60	mL	¼	c		chopped stuffed olives
60	mL	¼	c		seedless dark raisins
15	mL	1	T		vinegar
2	mL	½	t		crushed red pepper
500	mL	2	c		white cornmeal
125	mL	½	c		butter
750	mL	3	c		water
1		1			egg, slightly beaten
					salt

Method:

1. Pour cornmeal into boiling salted water. Add butter, stir and cook for 10 minutes. Remove from heat, add egg and stir well. Line bottom and sides of a well-greased ovenproof pan with mixture.

2. Meanwhile, saute onions and garlic in a skillet until golden brown. Add green pepper, tomatoes, parsley and vinegar. Cook over low heat about 10 minutes. Add remaining ingredients, blending well. Pour into cornmeal lined pan.

3. Cover with aluminum foil, and bake in a 180°C (350°F) oven for about 30 minutes. Serve hot.

VIETNAM

Location: Asia
Capital City: Hanoi
Language: Vietnamese, French
Monetary Unit: Dong

VIETNAMESE FRIED RICE
Servings: 4

Ingredients:

1	L	4	c	cooked rice
3		3		eggs, beaten
15	mL	1	T	fish sauce
30	mL	2	T	vegetable oil
30	mL	2	T	onion, minced
125	mL	½	c	Chinese sausages, cubed
60	mL	¼	c	crab meat, finely flaked
125	mL	½	c	scallions with green part, chopped

Method:

1. Pour oil into hot wok or skillet over medium heat. Stir in onion, sausages and crab meat. Cook about 1 minute. Add rice, stirring rapidly, and cook until thoroughly heated. Do not brown.

2. Make a well in centre of rice and add egg and fish sauce, stirring constantly. When eggs have a soft scrambled consistency, start incorporating rice, stirring in a circular fashion. When rice and eggs are blended, add scallion and serve immediately.

   Fish sauce and Chinese sausage can be found at any Oriental store.

YEMEN ARAB REPUBLIC

Location: Asia
Capital City: Sanaa
Language: Arabic
Monetary Unit: Yemen Riyal

VERMICELLI WITH LAMB
Servings: 4

Ingredients:

500	g	1	lb	stewing lamb, cut into small pieces
30	mL	2	T	oil
1		1		Spanish onion, sliced
60	mL	4	t	tomato paste
500	mL	2	c	hot water
250	mL	1	c	vermicelli, grain shaped (orzo)
500	mL	2	c	hot water
30	mL	2	T	butter
				salt
				black pepper

Method:

1. In a saucepan, brown meat in oil, then add onion. Saute until onion is golden brown. Add tomato paste, salt, pepper and hot water. Cover pan, reduce heat and simmer until water is evaporated and meat is tender.

2. Meanwhile, saute vermicelli in butter in a skillet for about 4 minutes. Add hot water and salt. Bring to a boil, then simmer until water is evaporated.

3. Put vermicelli in a serving dish and place meat mixture over it. Serve hot.

YUGOSLAVIA

Location: Europe
Capital City: Belgrade
Language: Serbo-Croatian, Slovenian, Turkish
Monetary Unit: Dinar

LAMB IN YOGURT SAUCE
Servings: 6

Ingredients:

1	kg	2	lb	lamb, cut into large pieces
30	mL	2	T	flour
3		3		eggs
750	mL	3	c	yogurt
1		1		onion, chopped
45	mL	3	T	oil
125	mL	½	c	water
				salt
				pepper

Method:

1. Season meat with salt and pepper and saute in oil with onion until light brown. Add water and cook over low heat with lid on until tender.

2. Place meat in a greased baking dish and set aside.

3. Beat egg yolks and blend in yogurt, flour, salt and pepper. Whisk egg whites until stiff and fold into yogurt mixture. Pour mixture over meat and cook in a 180°C (350°F) oven until sauce thickens.

ZIMBABWE

Location: Africa
Capital City: Harare
Language: English, Sindebele
Monetary Unit: Zimbabwean Dollar

ZIMBABWEAN STEW
Servings: 6

Ingredients:

1	kg	2 lb	stewing beef
125	mL	½ c	flour
60	mL	4 T	butter
			salt
			pepper
2		2	medium onion, sliced
800	mL	28 oz	can tomatoes
15	mL	1 T	sugar
			salt
			paprika
			cayenne pepper

Method:

1. Dredge meat with flour, salt and pepper mixture. Sear in butter until brown.

2. Place all ingredients except sugar in a Dutch oven. Cover and simmer until meat is tender. Add sugar 15 minutes before stew is done.

3. Serve with boiled rice.

Index 1: Recipes By Titles

Index 2: Recipes By Classification

Hot chicken stew, 40
Iraqi kebabs, 60
Italian veal stew, 63
Jamaican rice, 65
Lamp and chicken rice, 43
Lamp and seafood stew, 114
Lamb in yogurt sauce, 127
Lentil shepherd's pie, 104
Liberian rice, 74
Liver dumplings, 76
Meat and vegetable stew, 29
Meat and vegetable tortillas, 39
Meat stew, 88
Meat turnovers, 11
Mutton tongues, 21
Nicaraguan rice, 87
Noodles with mushrooms, 94
Okra stew with lamb, 107

Salads and Side Dishes
Avocado salad, 49
Bean salad, 38
Bean fritters, 26
Bulgur wheat salad, 62
Cornmeal porridge, 78
Green mashed potato, 68
Green salad, 59
Herring salad, 55
Leek with rice, 8
Potato salad, 44
String beans salad, 123

Desserts
Afghani pudding, 7
Baked egg custard, 99
Banana fritters, 64
Flour dessert, 84
Kiwi chantilly, 86
Kuwaitian dessert, 70
Maple syrup pie, 25
Papaya wedges, 13
Pineapple cake, 108
Pineapple surprise, 14
Prague cake, 33
Pumpkin patties, 27
Sweet potato cake, 52
Trifle, 121

Beverages
Almond milkshake, 83
Calypso punch, 115
Ginger beer, 10
Irish coffee, 61

Breads
Lebanese bread-pita, 72
Olive bread, 32
Spoon bread, 122

Sauces
Coconut milk, 71
Dill sauce, 109
Lemon-garlic marinade, 77
Tahini dressing, 59
Wine-spice marinade, 77

Index 3: Suggested Menus

3.1 Shrimp soup with lime
cheese and onion pie
salad
fresh fruit

3.2 Lentil soup
iraqi kebab
bulgur pilaff
kiwi chantilly

3.3 Stuffed mussels
veal in dill sauce
boiled potatoes
fresh fruit and cheese

3.4 Potato soup
fish and shrimp stew
avacado salad
maple syrup pie

3.5 Chickpea soup
lentil shepherd's pie
salad
afghani pudding

3.6 Cream of peanut soup
chicken with rice
avocado salad
banana fritters

3.7 Lentil soup
liver dumplings
potato salad
sweet potato cake

3.8 Cheese souffle
lamp in yogurt sauce
french fried potatoes
papaya wedges

3.9 Black-bean soup
rolled veal cutlets
green mashed potato
pineapple surprise

3.10 Black-bean soup
meat and vegetable tortillas
avocado salad
baked egg custard

3.11 Fish roe dip
spinach stew
rice pilaff
pineapple cake

3.12 Meatball soup
filafel
green salad
pumpkin patties

3.13 Bean salad
romanian hamburger
leek with rice
fresh fruit

3.14 Spring rolls
braised chicken with pork
omani rice
kiwi chantilly

3.15 Herring salad
bean millet pumpkin stew
spoon bread
ice cream

3.16 Potato soup
crab meat omelets
tossed salad
pumpkin patties

3.17 Lentil soup
eggplant casserole
omani rice
fresh fruit

3.18 Cream of peanut soup
mutton tongues
string beans salad
prague cake

3.19 Fish pudding
baked potatoes
cole slaw
maple syrup pie with ice
cream

3.20 Cheese souffle
sea bass casserole
green salad
trifle